UNITE
and
Conquer

UNITE
and
Conquer

• • •

How to Build Coalitions That Win—and Last

Kyrsten Sinema

Berrett-Koehler Publishers, Inc.
San Francisco
a BK Currents book

Berrett-Koehler Publishers, Inc.
235 Montgomery Street, Suite 650
San Francisco, CA 94104-2916
Tel: (415) 288-0260   Fax: (415) 362-2512   www.bkconnection.com

Ordering Information
Quantity sales. Special discounts are available on quantity purchases by corporations, associations, and others. For details, contact the "Special Sales Department" at the Berrett-Koehler address above.

Individual sales. Berrett-Koehler publications are available through most bookstores. They can also be ordered directly from Berrett-Koehler: Tel: (800) 929-2929; Fax: (802) 864-7626; www.bkconnection.com.
Orders for college textbook/course adoption use. Please contact Berrett-Koehler: Tel: (800) 929-2929; Fax: (802) 864-7626.

Orders by U.S. trade bookstores and wholesalers. Please contact Ingram Publisher Services: Tel: (800) 509-4887; Fax: (800) 838-1149; E-mail: customer.service@ingram publisherservices.com; or visit www.ingrampublisherservices.com/Ordering for details about electronic ordering.

Berrett-Koehler and the BK logo are registered trademarks of Berrett-Koehler Publishers, Inc.

Printed in the United States of America

Berrett-Koehler books are printed on long-lasting acid-free paper. When it is available, we choose paper that has been manufactured by environmentally responsible processes. These may include using trees grown in sustainable forests, incorporating recycled paper, minimizing chlorine in bleaching, or recycling the energy produced at the paper mill.

Library of Congress Cataloging-in-Publication Data
Sinema, Kyrsten.
 Unite and conquer : how to build coalitions that win and last / Kyrsten Sinema. — 1st ed.
  p. cm.
 Includes index.
 ISBN 978-1-57675-889-2 (pbk. : alk. paper)
 1. Coalitions—United States. 2. Politics, Practical—United States. I. Title.
JK1726.S58   2009
324.0973—dc22   2009012491

FIRST EDITION
14 13 12 11 10 09   10 9 8 7 6 5 4 3 2 1

Cover design by Mark van Bronkhorst
Cover photo by Mark Duran
Interior design and composition by Beverly Butterfield, Girl of the West Productions
Copyediting by PeopleSpeak
Indexing by Rachel Rice

• • • This book is dedicated to everyone working to make their corner of the world just a little bit better.

CONTENTS

FOREWORD

During my time as governor of Arizona, there were many instances where I was at an event and someone would lean over to me and whisper "I'm a Republican, but I voted for you."

They had to be out there. I was elected three times—once as attorney general and twice as governor—as a Democrat in a state where Democratic support alone can't win you an election.

The key to making change in politics is to give those types of people a home—to enlarge the circle, include people who may not agree with you on everything, and make skeptics into partners. This can be difficult, but the larger and more diverse the coalition, the greater the potential to achieve common goals. This has been one of my priorities during my time in politics. I try at every turn to think about how I can reach a wider array of people who may have an interest in a common vision and bring them together.

That's the imperative at the center of *Unite and Conquer,* where Kyrsten Sinema describes her experience putting together winning coalitions—at the ballot box and in the legislature—against long odds.

Kyrsten is one of the greatest characters in Arizona politics today, but she is also one of its least likely success stories. As Kyrsten explains, if you had met her when she first ran for the legislature, you would not have believed that someone so suspicious of those who disagreed with her, and someone with political beliefs so unconventional for Arizona, would help to leave a tangible mark on the state's politics just a few years later. Anyone who has thought about getting involved in politics but then thought "I don't have the chance to do anything important" should pay close attention.

As Kyrsten demonstrates, during a career in politics, everyone grows. You think about your past experiences, learn lessons, and apply them to situations you encounter in the future. This has certainly been true in my own case.

The key in this process of growing is to remember the touchstone of your involvement: why you got involved in the first place. This imperative encourages people to stay true to their beliefs—but it also can discourage compromise or working with potential adversaries, the kind of activities that make change happen in reality.

The tension between doing what's needed to accomplish tangible change and staying true to one's beliefs—the clash between ideology and practicality—is a tough line to walk. And to someone just beginning in organizing, the challenges of putting together a winning coalition can be daunting. In this book, Kyrsten helps make that a bit easier. Few people turn from a gadfly member of the legislature into an effective organizer. But that is Kyrsten's story—and this book contains not just the account of how that happened but also the lessons she took from that experience. She learned over the course of several terms in the legislature so you can learn over the course of a few hundred pages.

The greatest need for any person trying to make meaning-ful change in his or her community is other people—whether they're voters whispering in your ear or legislative colleagues across the aisle giving your position a fair hearing. No one can do it alone. Here, Kyrsten has written a practical blue-print that's a must-read for those who feel the need to change their communities through the political process. But she is also one of the first to explain, in nuts-and-bolts terms, the workings of our country's new type of politics—a poli-tics where diverse people unite behind common goals, where leaders are willing to put aside small differences for the sake of the big picture, and where unity replaces divi-sion as the key to great leadership.

In the past, efforts to describe the essence of politics have re-sounded with cynicism. Politics is likened to sausage making or cat herding; it is called the organization of grievance, or the process by which people who once had good intentions sell out for expediency.

But the political phenomena that have changed our coun-try in the last few years—foremost among these President Obama's historic rise to the White House—have given us a less cynical and more hopeful model for what politics really is: the organization of people with common interests and con-cerns and the act of mobilizing them toward a common goal.

We have seen the ability of broad-based, well-led coalitions to change politics and empower people who had never thought they could make much of a difference. And that's what this book is truly about.

The lessons in this book about empowerment replacing cynicism emerge from Kyrsten's own experience. The "side-line" approach to politics that she describes as typical of her early legislative career is one characterized by doubt. It comes from a feeling that you're powerless to make meaningful change in a political process swirling around you.

This is a volume full of practical advice for those who have ever felt that sensation but who also feel the need to make a difference through the political process. Kyrsten intelligently discusses all the important questions for idealists at work in politics today: how to compromise without compromising your beliefs, how to disagree without being disagreeable, how to take people who differ on many issues and inspire them toward common goals, and how to lead people in a way that is simultaneously successful in the rough-and-tumble world of politics and true to the core beliefs of the participants.

Kyrsten's book provides the kind of practical advice that makes the difference between a starry-eyed idealist on the sidelines and a seasoned idealist enacting meaningful change. There are millions of people who might whisper to you "We may not agree on everything, but I supported you on this issue"—and those are the type of interactions that will empower more people in the political process and bring needed change to our communities.

Janet Napolitano
Governor of Arizona, 2003–2009

PREFACE

I didn't set out to write a book, but this exciting and somewhat scary endeavor came to me in the form of an irresistible offer to share what I've been working on, talking about, and teaching others to do for several years. Here's how it happened. Around January of 2008, I was invited to speak at the 2008 Take Back America Conference in Washington, DC. I accepted the invitation, bought a plane ticket, and put together a PowerPoint presentation. Two months later, I found myself speaking to a large group of political activists, elected officials, and probably a few bloggers about Arizona Together, a statewide coalition formed to defeat a same-sex marriage ban initiative in Arizona.

You see, from January 2005 through November 2006, I had served as the chair of Arizona Together. It was a grueling two years full of challenges, internal questions, doubt, controversy, and incredible pressure to perform. As chair, my job was to guide the campaign every day toward victory, make strategic decisions about messaging, raise money, decide how to spend the money, direct community outreach efforts, and more. We won. And by *won,* I mean that we actually got more votes than the other guys. This was pretty exhilarating because no one wins these campaigns. And by *no one,* I literally mean no one. Activists have battled thirty of these initiatives around the country, and we have won only once. Lucky for me, it happened in Arizona. Since then, people around the country have wanted to know how we managed to do the impossible, and I have wanted to tell people how we did it. Hence my willingness to leave sunny, warm Arizona in the spring to travel to cold, wet Washington, DC.

So there I was at the conference, clicking through my Power-Point slides and telling the audience how we brought a bunch of disparate people together, formed a pretty massive coalition, raised some decent money, figured out how to talk to the voters, and worked our tails off for two years. The presentation was based on a thesis of our campaign—that we had to reach out to those voters who are different from ourselves (ourselves being the gay activists and traditional LGBT [lesbian, gay, bisexual, and transgender] allies) and speak a language relevant to their lives in order to build a base big enough and strong enough to win on election day. While this thesis sounds like a pretty good recipe for winning a ballot initiative campaign, it was not developed or executed without controversy, the same kind of controversy progressives have faced for years.

The question of whom we as progressive political actors will collaborate with is not an easy one to answer. Some believe that we should work with anyone and everyone to accomplish our higher goals (world peace, etc.) and that adjusting our language and the way we interact with each other and the world is a valuable exercise that helps us win and makes us stronger. Others believe that working with our natural base* is the only way to achieve success and that working with those who operate on a different plane (read: conservatives) is tantamount to selling out. Arizona Together chose the first route. It wasn't easy and we had some pretty bumpy times, but it worked.

You might be thinking, "Well, if the strategy worked, then it isn't very controversial, is it?" But, oh, it is—because another reader (and this might be you too, dear reader) is slowly shaking his or her head back and forth right now, thinking "That girl will do anything to win. What a shame." We've been dealing with this quandary for years, without any clear consensus about what exactly we should do and where, if anywhere, we should draw the line when working with disparate groups.

So, again, there I was talking to the progressive faithful about our controversial thesis—committing to working with people who are wildly different from me and learning to speak a new language to people who are different from me, all in order to protect health care for unmarried families in Arizona and stop the marriage ban—and I could feel some people in the room shooting me dark looks and muttering under their breath about sellout politicians. In such situations, I find that humor helps. It's hard to justify throwing things at the girl at the front of the room if she's just told a self-deprecating joke.

---

* The *base* is what politicians call their true believers. It usually includes you, your six best friends, and a handful of people just like you. Both the Left and the Right have their own base, which is slightly larger than my little description here—but not by much.

In fact, if the girl's tone is just right, the person gripping the rock or pen or little hotel glass cup holding cheap candy might actually relax that tight, sweaty grip on the object to be thrown and chuckle a little. I did what any girl would do at this point—I threw in a little humor. The speech ended, and a handful of people gathered around the dais to talk a bit more. I spent a few moments with each person, and then only one person was left. This editor looked at me, said something nice about the speech that I can't remember, and then asked me if I wanted to write a book about building coalitions.

And here we are.

The Beauty of Coalitions

I've been building coalitions all my life, although I didn't know to call them coalitions in the early years. When I was little, my parents told me I just talked too much and needed to mind my own business. In junior high, everybody thought I was just bossy. In high school, I called what I did organizing, and when I was preparing for a career in social work, I learned it was really coalition building.

To put it simply, coalition building is the practice of gathering disparate people and groups together for a common purpose or goal. The beauty of coalition-building is that everyone can come to the coalition full of his or her own values and ideals and not be asked or required to give up a single one of them. Not giving up values or ideals makes me happy because I am a bit stubborn about those sorts of things (as really most of us are). After all, I have some pretty good reasons for choosing these values and ideals, and I'm not giving them up for every attractive proposal that saunters by. Coalitions allow you to get important work done while being who you really want to be. They also have the great benefit of being bigger than just you, so the outcome of your work can also be much bigger than just the work you could accomplish on your own. And if you're a social animal like me, then they offer the bonus of getting to do great work in the company of other people doing great work.

For some of us, working in coalitions comes naturally. I took to it at an early age, probably due to my extraordinary interest in talking to people, and that included all people— everyone I saw. My early attempts included wandering away from my family at the Tucson Mall, hanging around another random family for a bit to see what they were up to, and eventually asking a mall security officer to help me find my own family again. The next attempt came in the first grade when I teamed up with another little girl after school one day to sell chocolate bars in the neighborhood to raise money for my big brother's soccer team. We sold every single bar in the box that afternoon* to the slightly surprised adults throughout the neighborhood and then headed

---

* Except for the one bar that we ate ourselves toward the end of the afternoon. All that walking and talking really tuckered us out. Plus, even at the age of six, I was addicted to chocolate.

home, only to find four police cars in the driveway. I'd neglected to tell anyone where my enterprising friend and I were going—or get permission to go in the first place.

While I showed some proclivity toward coalition building at a young age, I learned many of the finer points through trial and error over the years. In college, I studied social work, with the intention of changing the world, ending global hunger, and saving the environment, and I was hoping to get it all done within a year or two. Dissatisfaction set in almost immediately, when I found myself working as a school social worker in a deeply impoverished community and counting distributing food boxes among my greatest achievements. Working one-on-one with children and their families is incredibly important, but I found it quite depressing. I kept asking myself, "Couldn't I have a larger impact—couldn't I make a difference in the underlying structure that created this vicious cycle of poverty?" So I went back to school at night to earn a master's in social work, hoping that the extra training and knowledge would make me a more effective change agent. I learned lots of stuff like how to effectively organize in communities and create meaningful programs that impact people's lives, and I spent another six years organizing immigrant and refugee families in the community, creating and expanding empowerment programs, and lobbying the Arizona legislature for state reform.

Then in 2002 I felt like I'd really hit a wall. I'd done as much as my training and hyperactive mind allowed me to do, and it was time to move on. I met my friend Sandy Bahr for coffee, and by the end of the meeting, I'd made the decision to quit my job, get a law degree, and run for state office. I hoped that learning to think like a lawyer would help me get access to the power attorneys wield so I could wield some of that power for good. And I'd decided that serving in the state legislature would help me change some of those institutional barriers to success that I'd struggled with over the years. Along the way, I learned so much from other talented activists, organizers, and policy makers about how to work together and create lasting, meaningful change. We've been able to do some pretty great things for our little corner of the world over the years, and my intention in writing this book is to share some of those stories with you and explain how you might do them too.

I hope this book will illuminate some of the finer points of coalition building, and I've sprinkled a few stories throughout the book to illustrate the trials and errors of attempting coalition work. Now I'm a politician (wait! don't put the book down!), so in my world we expect everything to be short and snappy with the important stuff highlighted. You've already seen that this book is small, which I hope induced you to pick it up and flip through it. I've done my best to make each chapter snappy—first by making my point, then by telling a story or two to illustrate the point, and then by adding some humor to make sure you don't get bored. And finally, the important stuff is easy to find. I've got nifty little text boxes throughout the book, highlighting some of the parts that you can read in a jiffy and then use in the real world.

Sneak Preview

And now I'll give you a quick preview of the whole book in case you're reading this the night before you start your first community organizing job and you're panicking because you might have overstated your experience and, in fact, don't know what on earth to do. Or maybe you're a veteran coalition builder and aren't sure that there's anything in this book that you don't already know. Perhaps you just bought the book for the pretty purple cover (I totally would) and now are in the process of deciding whether it's actually worth reading. Whatever your reason, here's the preview:

In the introduction, "Because You Can't Get There on Your Own," I introduce the concept of coalition building, what brought me to it in my current incarnation as an elected official, and why working in coalition with other people is the greatest thing since sliced bread. Chapter 1, "The Politics We Want," describes what's gone wrong with politics lately and why Americans hate politics and politicians (except perhaps Barack Obama). The chapter outlines the kind of politics we really want and proposes a trans-formation to a new ethos that can guide our political thoughts and behavior to get us the politics we want. Chapter 2, "Letting Go of the Bear and Picking Up the Buddha," teaches the steps to transforming politics from the tired old style of pettiness to a new style rooted in a place of peace, motivated by the genuine desire to do good, and tempered with individual awareness and centeredness. Chapter 3, "Creating Coalitions You Actually Want to Join," covers the important steps required to build coalitions that people want to be a part of, points out common pitfalls to coalition building, and discusses the vital role of leadership in coalitions. In chapter 4, "Shedding the Heavy Mantle of Victimhood," I jump right into the lion's den with the controversial proposal that we dump identity politics—the practice of dividing up into subgroups based on some aspect of shared identity—and instead focus on the larger truth that we all share most things in common and want mostly the same things out of life.* Chapter 5, "Making Friends," is one of my favorite chapters. It stresses the importance of making friends when setting out to build a meaningful coalition and provides a guide for readers to use when making friends. In chapter 6, "Letting Go of Outcomes," we explore what outcomes are, why we're so attached to them, and how this attachment gets in the way of finding effective solutions in coalition settings. Chapter 7, "Getting Back to Our Shared Values," brings us back to what we as Americans can all share—our core values. This chapter illustrates that when we use values-based language, we can attract more people to the table to work together and then provides examples of how to create and use values-based language. Chapter 8, "Naming Our Interests," explains what an interest is and how it is different from an outcome, then discusses how naming interests helps guide our coalition work to shared successful outcomes that everyone can embrace. Chapter 9, "The Third Way," illustrates just how a coalition's work can be successful when coalition members eschew

----

* Money and fame, right?

identity politics; create meaningful, trust-based relationships; let go of predetermined outcomes; name shared values; and then use interest-based work to create and execute the coalition's plan. Chapter 10, "And, Not But," proposes the elimination of the word *but* from our coalition vocabulary and submits the word *and* in its place. By using the word *and* when working with diverse people and groups around the coalition table, we can decrease unnecessary arguments, increase creativity, and move faster and more powerfully toward real solutions that meet everyone's needs. In chapter 11, "Keeping the Team Together," I discuss three tools coalition builders can and should use to keep the coalition together and working for a common purpose. In the conclusion, "Get Your Coalition On," I wrap up the lessons from the book and set you, the reader, forth to unite and conquer. And at the very end of this little book, you'll find a bonus "Coalition Builder's Toolkit" that describes the method I use when running (and winning) campaigns in a coalition setting.

There's the preview for this book. I hope it was tempting and juicy because the real book starts when you turn the page, and it would be a shame to skip all that.

INTRODUCTION

Because You Can't Get There on Your Own

I kind of fell into this whole legislator gig. I didn't really intend to run for office, but as a school social worker in the late 1990s, working with immigrant and refugee kids in poverty, I found myself spending more and more time at the state capitol as time went on. I was often frustrated that these kids weren't getting the same opportunities that I had as a child or that other children in our state had access to, and I thought that lobbying was my best shot at getting something for these kids. Well, I didn't make a whole lot of headway in that respect, but I did learn about state politics. I was kind of surprised—I'd always assumed that legislators were somehow different from the rest of us. But it turns out that they're just regular people.

What I didn't like is that not enough of those regular people seemed to care about the things that I cared about—like affordable health care for kids; good, strong schools with equal opportunity; clean air and water; and investments in the future via smart growth and economic development. So after a while, I decided I'd run for office.

I was elected in November 2004 to represent District 15 in central Phoenix, an urban district that cares about education, health care, and the environment. Going into my first legislative sessions, I felt pretty confident that I'd represent the interests of my constituents well—after all, I told them what I believed in, and they'd elected me to serve them. I showed up to the capitol quite bright-eyed and bushy-tailed, ready to take the state by storm.

Except it didn't quite work out like that. I showed up all right. And for the first several months, I was bright-eyed and bushy-tailed, coming to work every morning full of vim and vigor, ready to face off for justice—which made me rather annoying. I'd stand up four or five times a week on the floor of the house and give scathing speeches about how this bill and that bill were complete and utter travesties of justice, and the paper would capture one or two of the quotes, and then we'd vote on the offending bills and they'd pass with supermajorities. I'd get righteously indignant and head back to my office, incensed that my colleagues could not only write but actually support and vote for such horrid policies!

Meanwhile, everyone else went to lunch. In short, my first legislative session was a bust. I'd spent all my time being a crusader for justice, a patron saint for lost causes, and I'd missed out on the opportunity to form meaningful relationships with fellow members in the legislature, lobbyists, and other state actors. I hadn't gotten any of my great policy ideas enacted into law, and I'd seen lots of stuff I didn't like become law. It was just plain sad.

I spent the summer figuring out what I wanted to change. I knew that I couldn't keep doing what I was doing because it wasn't working for me and I hated it. I had, without actually planning to do so, fallen quite easily into the role of the loyal opposition, the righteously indignant crusader, the bomb thrower. In legislative lingo, a bomb thrower is a legislator who chooses to yell from the sidelines, cackle at the rest of the body, and generally raise hell from the corner of the room. A person who chooses to be a bomb thrower in the legislature is choosing to remove himself or herself from the work of the body: negotiating on bills, working to find compromises, and sometimes teaming up with unusual allies to promote or kill legislation. This person plays an important role at the capitol because he or she calls out the body on a regular basis (which is needed, especially considering that the general public hears or reads roughly 0.3 percent of what happens each day inside the legislature). However, the bomb thrower has made a choice—whether consciously or not—to be excluded from the actual process of negotiating proposed legislation. You can't play both roles in the legislature; if you choose to be a bomb thrower, you will not get the opportunity to amend bills, participate in bipartisan meetings to craft good legislation, or work with people on the other side of the aisle to kill bad legislation. I unwittingly chose to be a bomb thrower my first session, which led to my unhappiness and regret.

Over the summer, I consciously chose to reject the bomb thrower role. For me, it was not a hard choice to make. I was miserable as a bomb thrower. And since I hadn't consciously chosen that role, I was even more depressed when I realized that I had become a bomb thrower and worked my way right into that lonely corner. It didn't fit me. I do love to give fiery speeches. But I also love people. I love talking with people, working together, and making friends. The bomb thrower doesn't get to make friends much (understandably so), and she certainly doesn't get to work with all the people she's throwing bombs toward.

I reflected on the lessons I'd learned as a social worker—about meeting people where they are, forming trust-based relationships, and working with others to create a realistic plan of action that gets you toward your goal. My social worker skills had served me well over the years, and I thought I'd try them at the capitol. I knew that I wouldn't be successful all the time (after all, Arizona's legislature is controlled by the other party in both the house and the senate, and Democrats rarely passed bills with their names attached), but I figured I'd be at least marginally more successful (there's only one way to go up from zero) and certainly a lot happier. So I took the advice that I'd ignored the year before from my state senator, Ken Cheuvront,[1] and started over. When I went back to the legislature a few months later, it was like a whole different world had opened for me.

I calmed down and stopped taking everything so personally, which made me a lot nicer and, I think, reduced the furrowing of my brow. I made friends with Democrats, Republicans, and everyone in between, which made me a lot happier. I had meetings with lobbyists that were relaxed and comfortable (regardless of whether or not we agreed on an issue). I laughed with legislators both liberal and conservative. I accepted losses with greater grace, participated in a few wins, and started getting invitations from Republican legislators to work together on bills.

It's not all fun and roses—sometimes it's still really, really hard to be in the legislature, and some days I still wonder why anyone would do this job[2]—but for the most part, I'm glad that I'm there, and I'm glad that I get lots done. It took four steps for me to get to the place I am now—where I can work well with just about anyone and where I can form and operate in coalitions that are some of the most unlikely you've ever heard about. First, it took recognition on my part that I didn't like where I was or what I was doing and recognition that it could be different and I could make it so. Second, it took some personal transformation. I had to change the way I thought and behaved so I could see other people and reach out to them and work effectively. Third, it took relationship building. I had to make friends and find common ground with people who were sometimes very, very different from me. I had to build trust with them and allow them to build trust with me. And fourth, it took strategic work where we'd all put aside our own preconceived ideas of how to solve the world's problems and instead use our shared values to create plans that worked for everyone.

Not only did these four steps change the way that I work at the capitol, in the community, and around the nation, they helped my work matter. Thanks to my ever-developing coalition-building skills, I've been able to be a part of some really exciting and meaningful change in this country—from protecting health care for families to fighting genocide to supporting diversity in higher education and more.

I probably could have found other ways to fill my time as a legislator without seeking out and forming coalitions, but I'm thinking that would have been horrid. My first year in the legislature sure was. Going it alone is no fun, plus there's no one to invite to the victory party. Coalitions, on the other hand, are challenging, hard, exhilarating and rewarding, and ultimately lead to a larger concept of winning. That sounds like a pretty good party to me.

The Politics We Want

What kind of world do we want? As progressives, we believe in fairness and justice. We think that all people are equal and should be treated as such, and we think that everyone should be respected for who he or she is. We believe in open processes where everyone is treated with dignity. We value freedom—both freedom from tyranny and the freedom to be and do what we dream. We want everyone to have the opportunity to succeed. And we believe in responsibility—for ourselves, for each other, and for the earth. Finally, we believe in love as a driving force for humanity.

We want to live in a paradise where all of our values have a place, so let's identify what our vision for the world really is and embrace an ethos that is true to our core values. Instead of falling for the tricks and old habits from the past, when we allowed fear and division to rule our decisions, we instead will choose a better path. This "new ethos"—this way of living and doing—simply means that we're choosing to live and act in accordance with our values. This means that we practice what we want to achieve.

Old School

The old-school handbook of politics says that the best way to beat your opponents is to use their own tricks against them. If they've been running commercials that bash your candidate and make her look bad (even though they're not quite true), then we should run commercials that bash their candidate and make him look bad (even if they're not quite true).

The old-school handbook of politics says that the best way to win an issue is to outfox your opponents—trick them into something or go around them to get what you want. In the old-school handbook, political actors seek ways to overpower or outmaneuver each other.

The old-school handbook of politics is about scheming and plotting—how to get what you want from the political process while making the other guy look bad. How to one-up his press release or media stunt from the other day. How to look smart, benevolent, and charming while your opponent looks like someone who would literally steal from a child.

It's easy to see why so many people hate politics.

The old-school handbook of politics, quite simply, continues political action in the vein it's been traveling in over the past forty years. Cooperation and collaboration are rare, especially when the issue is very important. Partisan-ship is valued as being true to the ideals of one political party. People do not reach across the aisle to work together, much less create friendships together.

Back in the super old days (*before* the "old-school politics" days), Congress was different. Members worked together more frequently on bipartisan legislation, and party registration was not a prerequisite to friendships or invitations to after-work gatherings. Lee Hamilton served in the United States House for nearly thirty-four years and once wrote that he watched Hubert Humphrey and Barry Goldwater duke it out on the floor of the Senate, then leave after work to have a drink together.[1] Today, such relationships are rare. In fact, those elected officials who do manage to maintain close friendships with members from the opposite party are often viewed as sellouts or are not trusted within their caucus because of their cozy relationship with "the other side."

These kinds of deep divisions have hurt our ability to practice politics in a way that is uplifting and worthwhile. Instead, they've reduced us to the lowest common denominator, causing politics to reflect trashy daytime talk shows ("Watch *Jerry Springer* today to see which member of Congress reveals a shocking secret about his suitemate that you'll be *wild* to hear!") that interest few and engage even fewer.

Sadly, this is pretty much how politics operates today—on both sides of the aisle. Many credit the 1994 "Contract with America" campaign, the brainchild of Newt Gingrich, with ushering in a hyperpartisanship that has become standard fare in American politics. During the 1994 congressional election cycle, the Contract with America laid out specific policy proposals by the Republican House caucus. All but two sitting Republican House members signed the contract, and every single Republican House candidate in the country signed it prior to the election.[2] After Republicans took a majority in the House, they began passing bills based on the proposals in the contract. Most of the bills never made it through the Senate or became law, but their very existence as items for debate changed the way in which members of Congress worked together (or, more appropriately, didn't work together). Gone were the days of hashing out the elements of a bill in a bipartisan work group—instead, wholesale ideas created by one party were brought to the floor and ushered through. This brand of politics has made a lasting impression on our nation. Now that Democrats have reclaimed the House, we read regular reports from Republicans decrying the Democrats' unwillingness to create legislation in a bipartisan fashion. Instead, they say, the Democrats create legislation in a back room somewhere and then push it through the floor, regardless of the views of the minority party.

Americans are quite clearly sick of the old-school practice of politics. Voters say regularly that they're tired of the partisan bickering and want politicians to sit down and work out practical solutions to the pressing problems facing our country. While we hear this regularly from the public, we've not made any real effort to change the way we do business, and so the hyperpartisanship continues. But I believe that in order to survive politically in the coming years, we as progressives must find a new way to engage in politics— one that is true to the values that we espouse and that strives to emulate the kind of world that we actually want to live in.

A New Ethos

What can we do differently? I propose that we choose instead to engage in politics from a belief that you must practice politics in a way that you would like politics to be. Even if the prevailing attitude about political activity demands that you engage in smear tactics against your opponents, you reject that method of acting and instead choose a higher road of engagement that focuses on finding common ground with those typically considered opponents and that seeks to create solutions that meet everyone's interests. You put aside the inflammatory rhetoric about those who are different from you and seek to highlight that which affects us all and can bring us together.

President Barack Obama's campaign for the United States presidency was a phenomenon, sweeping the country like wildfire. Democrats, Independents, even Republicans, became fans and supporters of Obama in numbers and with an intensity never before seen in my lifetime. While there's been no definitive study on this phenomenon, many credit his tsunami of support and, frankly, devotion to his unique brand of politics. During the primary election, Obama talked about bringing people together, downplayed conflicts between Americans, and said that we are all more alike than we are different. He said that there was no red America or blue America but one America. His campaign focused on hope and unity and an attempt to bring people together regardless of their political affiliation, race, age, gender, or geographic location. The word *transcend* has been used so often in connection with Obama that it's taken on almost mythic proportions.

While critics claim that Obama is a stock liberal (because his political views on policy issues are pretty typically progressive), what has made him different from other major candidates in recent years is his willingness and his comfort with difference, as well as his refusal to concede that divisions must be standard fare in party politics. While this has made him appealing to independents and even some conservatives, its effect, I think, has been most impactful among the left—who for years have sounded angry and bitter when part of the national discourse.

Barack Obama embraced the new ethos—his speeches, day after day, centered on what brings Americans together and downplayed what separates us. He repeated, in varying iterations, that "the choice in this election is not between regions or religions or genders. It's not about rich versus poor; young versus old; and it is not about black versus white. It's about the past versus the future."[3] By speaking a message of unity and hope, he invigorated an until-then-dormant American public and inspired millions of people to engage in politics anew.

But while Obama is a great poster child for the new ethos of politics, one doesn't need his oratory skills or charisma to actually practice this ethos. Instead, ordinary Americans the country over can (and I argue, should) begin practicing the new ethos in city councils, on school boards, in legislatures, and in political coalitions of all stripes. By putting aside partisan and hackneyed tactics that rely on obfuscation, trickery, domination, and plain old bullying and instead finding common ground with others and embracing a commitment to shared outcomes, we can transform politics to reflect a more progressive vision of the world and, in the bargain, accomplish a whole lot more while at it.

The Transformation

How do we move from a politics based on fear and domination to a politics based on unity and shared values? We cannot get there by waiting for others to take us there. We cannot expect that this new ethos of politics will materialize, and we can simply join it and take our spot at the table. We must create it ourselves. That means taking the risk to be the one who engages others—those who are different from us—and forms relationships, builds trust, and finds common ground. It means being willing to take some political lumps from our own party and fellow ideologues. It means being ready to try something new and untested—that pundits will warn you against.

In the fall of 2008, I was running for reelection to the state house of representatives in Arizona. I'd served two terms and was asking the voters to return me for a third term. As is common in most local elections, all the candidates in the race were invited to participate in a debate. My Democratic colleague in the house, David Lujan, and I attended (in Arizona, each district has two state representatives, both elected at-large), as did our Republican challenger. Roughly six members of the public attended (which is also pretty common in local elections). Over the course of an hour and a half, we answered questions from a moderator on a number of subjects ranging from the ever-growing budget deficit facing our state to immigration to education. The debate went well (at least the six attendees appeared to think it did), and at the end of it, a constituent came up to me and said, "Sinema, you don't even sound like a liberal anymore." I laughed and mentioned that I'd learned so much over the past four years; that I just wanted to find good, common-sense, practical solutions to our state's problems; and that I was done with the fiery rhetoric I started with. As we parted ways, I told the voter that I believed in all the progressive values that I'd always held dear, but I'd finally learned to talk about my values and beliefs in a way that created space for compromise and coalition.

As I drove home from the debate, I reflected more on his comment. I really had changed so much over the last four years—from the way that I thought to the way that I behaved and spoke. You see, I'd been convinced early on that the best way to engage in politics was to unequivocally highlight the *differences* between me and others, which led me quickly to isolation and irrelevance. Once I switched my thinking to a new ethos, not only was I able to open up lines of communication with those who are different from me, I was, more importantly, able to open up my own ways of thinking to embrace a much larger possibility than the strict party-line rhetoric I'd been using. And the difference has been stark. By acknowledging that my colleagues, both more liberal and more conservative than I, have ideas and values worth examining and sharing, I've been able to find common ground, make coalitions, and accomplish more than I ever anticipated to be possible.

And—perhaps most importantly—I've been much happier.

Here's a story illustrating the great success that can result from working in coalition with others.

In August 2005, I woke one day to read an article in the paper about a young mother who had been kicked out of a community pool area in Chandler (a suburb of Phoenix) for committing the heinous act of breast-feeding her baby at a table near the pool, under a blanket, while fully clothed.[4] It's easy to see why the city pool managers felt that it was only appropriate to kick her out of the pool area. Why, at a pool where people of all ages are frolicking in the water, lounging in the sun, and wandering around finding lost children (all while wearing bathing suits), it is shocking to think that any mother would consider putting a large blanket over her body, tucking her baby underneath, and discreetly feeding him.

This young mother had more fabric covering her and her baby's bodies than the rest of the pool-goers' clothing combined that day. Yet someone thought it was indecent for her to be seen feeding her child.

I was incensed, so I went online and tried to find her. After a week or so of e-mailing various people, I found Amy Milliron. I called Amy on the phone and volunteered to help her get a bill passed to protect all Arizona mothers who breast-feed their babies. This was quite an audacious offer, considering the fact that (1) Democrats don't typically get bills passed in the Arizona legislature and (2) other Democrats had introduced legislation to protect breast-feeding mothers for the prior eight years without ever getting a single hearing on the idea.

I was determined to help Amy—and I knew we could pass this law if we did it right. Throughout the fall of 2005 I met regularly with Amy and her fellow "lactivists," crafting legislation that would exempt breast-feeding mothers from indecent exposure statutes (laws that make it a crime to get naked on the street, etc.) and give them the legal right to breast-feed in public places without harassment. By December 2005, we'd crafted a pretty good bill. We just had to get it passed.

We decided on a two-pronged strategy. First, I'd make sure that Amy and her team of lactivists learned how to lobby effectively and support the legislation throughout the session. We reviewed the legislative process, covering everything from how a bill is introduced to when and where committees meet and how to talk to legislators about an issue. I taught them how to testify in committee, and we worked together to frame the issue in a way that would appeal to conservative members of the legislature. Amy and the moms agreed to get other breast-feeding moms around the state energized about the legislation so we'd have an army of e-mail and phone support for the bill once it was introduced.[5] We agreed to stay in constant contact as the bill proceeded so Amy and the other dozen or so moms on her team could show up at the capitol at any time to help the bill if the situation got sticky.

The second prong was my job: get the bill introduced, heard in committee, and passed on to the governor. I was just returning for my second year in the legislature, and I hadn't had much success the year before. I knew that I couldn't introduce the bill under my name because that would be the kiss of death. (My reputation as a bomb thrower was still fresh in people's minds.) I started the hunt for a sponsor, someone who would carry the bill but work with me to get it passed and stay true to Amy's intent. During the first week of session, Representative Jonathon Paton asked me about the bill. He'd read about Amy's story in the paper and was interested. Jonathon was a new legislator like me, but he— unlike me—is a Republican and had already formed good relationships with powerful Republican members of the legislature. He was a perfect choice to carry the bill. We quickly agreed that he would sponsor the bill in his name and work to get the bill a committee hearing and that I'd do the behind-the-scenes work of crafting the right kind of message and getting Amy and her team to lobby members of the legislature.

Jonathon got a hearing for the bill, and I prepped Amy and her team. Prior to the hearing, Amy and the lactivists e-mailed, called, and met in person with each committee member to talk about why the bill was needed. On the day of the committee hearing, Amy and two other moms testified in support of the bill. The framing was perfect—rather than talk about breast-feeding as a "women's rights" issue (which Democrats had done for years), they talked about a mother's need to take care of her baby (which Republicans can understand and connect with). Babies don't decide when to get hungry, but when they're hungry, everyone can hear it. Therefore, the hearing was all about moms doing their best to take care of their babies and keep them healthy and well-nourished. The framing worked, and the bill passed easily out of committee.

The next step was a full vote in the house of representatives. We were worried about a few of the very conservative members of the body opposing the bill—largely for reasons like modesty. So Amy and her team found politically conservative mothers who lived in the areas these members represented and asked the mothers to contact their representatives directly. The moms did an outstanding job—their e-mails and phone calls struck just the right tone. No longer was our breast-feeding bill a liberal bill about women's rights to bare their breasts in public; it was now a bill about respecting a mother's need to take care of her baby no matter where she happens to be. The bill passed nearly unanimously out of the house.

We moved to the senate and started the whole process over, using the same strategies and messages. Jonathon got the bill hearing set up, and I coached Amy and her team of moms in lobbying members and garnering support. When we encountered some resistance from a Democratic senator, I called him to answer his questions and gain his support. When the bill was stalled in the Senate Rules Committee, Jonathon visited with the committee chair to get the bill moving again. Throughout it all, Amy, Jonathon, and I triaged the bill on a nearly daily basis.

The bill ultimately passed with strong bipartisan support and was signed into law by the governor in the summer of 2006. It was my first major success at coalition work in the capitol, and it worked because I chose to let go of the old-school style of politics (which demanded that I see the

Republicans as an obstacle to overcome or foes to be defeated), find creative ways to work with others (like partnering with another new legislator from across the aisle), and learn new ways of talking to those who are different from me (by letting go of my lingo and speaking a language that fit the Republicans' worldview). In the chapters that follow, I'll discuss in greater detail the steps that I believe are critical to repeating coalition success over and over again.

BONUS BOX

What Is a Bonus Box?

At the end of each chapter, I've included these nifty text boxes for you to read very quickly and use in your political work. If your life is like mine—and in many ways, I dearly hope it is not[6]—then you're really busy. The bonus boxes are designed to recap a few of the tips, cautions, or ideas I hope you'll take away from each chapter—and to do so in a short, snappy form that you can glance at during a time of concern or crisis or in preparation for a coalition endeavor. Hopefully, this will let you do great work without having to rifle through the whole book each time you're setting out to change the world.

2

Letting Go of the Bear and Picking Up the Buddha

As progressives, we too often function from a gut-level reaction that is based on fear and anger, which limits our ability to truly engage in the kind of political activity that will lead us to the progressive world we want to live in. We need to learn how to recognize when we're engaging in politics from a place of fear or anger, and we need to shift to a place where we're centered—with ourselves, our work, and our relationships with others.

I don't think it's an easy task to alter the way we behave in politics, but I do believe that it can be done if we mindfully choose to make that alteration and then practice at it. I call this *letting go of the bear and picking up the Buddha.* The bear is the internal fight-or-flight reflex that we as humans are blessed to have. It can both save our lives and jeopardize our futures. *Putting down the bear* in your political practice occurs when you consciously choose not to act, react, or interact with others from a place of fear and uncertainty. *Picking up the Buddha* is code for being calm, cool, and collected—another ability that we humans have, although we often don't polish this political skill without some focused practice. Picking up the Buddha (becoming a super centered political actor) makes you a stronger, more effective you. To be your most fabulous political self, you'll need to recognize the bear and learn to let go of it in your work.

I call a centered place of politics *enso politics. Enso* is the Japanese word for *circle.* It symbolizes infinity, the perfect meditative state, and enlightenment. In politics, I think this translates to the political actor who engages in politics from a place of peace and serenity.

Rejecting the politics of fear, this chapter provides first an explanation of *why* enso politics is a more useful and productive tool for progressives, then provides a few quick tips to help you find your own way to practicing enso politics. As individuals, when we employ enso politics, we become more productive and happier change agents. We're less attached to our own ideas of what is right or wrong. We're more prepared to work with others across the political spectrum. Because we've let go of rigid ways of thinking and acting (and most often, reacting), we're ready to accept our colleagues as they are, and we're ready to work with each other as we bring whoever and whatever we are to the table.

Fight or Flight: A Great Way to Deal with Angry Bears

In the early years of human evolution, our species survived by using the core instinct of fight or flight in response to fear or threat. When confronted with a large flesh-eating animal, humans felt intense fear and then reflexively either ran or stayed to fight.[1] Our fight-or-flight instinct is quite useful, and I'm really glad that we humans have this tool in our bodies and brains. In 2008, we still need it. Although most of us aren't facing large flesh-eating animals daily, we do experience moments of intense fear and then must reflexively act to stay safe. During disasters like flash level 5 hurricanes or bridge collapses—or even tripping while running in four-inch stilettos (not that it's ever happened to me)—we need our fight-or-flight reflex. It literally saves our lives.

Fight or Flight: A Not So Great Way to Deal with People

The circumstances in which the fight-or-flight reflex serves us well aren't all that common anymore. More often, we face tough choices and difficult decisions that do not involve being eaten by a bear. Yet our bodies continue to express that fear reflex whenever we meet a significant challenge. And we tend to exercise our fight-or-flight response when that fear feeling is triggered. We either run from the problem or we lash out reflexively, seeking to protect ourselves from the impending threat.

Reacting like this is an ineffective way to engage in politics, yet it's pretty much our modus operandi in the progressive world. We decide that our candidate or our issue or our view of the world is the right one (because, of course, it is) and then we begin to run a campaign to persuade other people to see the candidate, issue, or view of the world in the same way that we do. This works just fine until someone disagrees with us about fifteen minutes into the campaign, and then the trouble starts. The moment someone attacks our candidate or issue, we fall back on our basic human instincts. What do we as progressives do when threatened? We feel fear. And then we react with a fight-or-flight response, counterattacking our opponents with information about their last affair or lies or whatever our private investigator could turn up about the other side. This behavior provokes fear in the hearts of listeners. And what do people do when they feel afraid? They kick into fight-or-flight mode and act reflexively to keep themselves safe. (They usually choose flight.) The entire voting public turns off the television because all they can see are two stupid politicians fighting over something no one really cares about: "These people don't care about my problems, and they're all corrupt anyway."

Not super effective, right? Yet we keep following this pattern over and over—usually because we haven't figured out another way to deal with politics the way it is practiced today. And because we haven't figured out another way, we keep reacting in the same way, which reinforces the cycle, and so it keeps going on and on.

The good news is that we can stop and change the way that we as individual actors engage in politics. We can learn to recognize the fight-or-flight reflex when it pops up and then consciously choose another path. That's the essence of enso politics—consciously choosing to engage in politics from a place of balance and centeredness.

Serenity Now!

My favorite character from *Seinfeld* was George Costanza's father. He yelled at the top of his lungs pretty much nonstop and was always in a rage about something. I love the episode where he was advised by his doctor to say "Serenity now" every time his blood pressure was about to go up— the idea being that this mantra would remind him to stay calm—and the rest of the episode he was shown screaming "Serenity now!" whenever things got tough or frustrating.[2] The idea was great; in practice, less great.

When you start practicing enso politics, you may feel like George's father. It's not easy to transition from the frantic, hectic, and often angry pace of politics to become a more relaxed, comfortable person who excels in political practice. But several steps can help you transition from screaming *"Serenity now!"* to calmly whispering "Serenity now."

Stop

Stop. That's it. Just stop—right in your tracks, as soon as you notice that you're blowing your top or your ears are turning red because you're so angry or that everyone around you in the war room is yelling and screaming about how horrible something is. Stop as soon as you notice that you're no longer feeling calm, cool, and in control.

Most people never notice that this shift in demeanor is even happening to them, so in order to stop, you first have to teach yourself to notice that you've drifted away from "normal" to a place of upset, stress, or anger. How do you notice this? Think right now of a time that you were angry or upset or flustered or scared.

- How did your body feel? Were your shoulders tense? Was your face hot? Was your heart beating fast? Remember the physical reactions that you were experiencing, what you were *feeling*, when you were upset, angry, or scared.

- What was going through your mind at the time? Was your mind racing? Was it a block of rage? Did the room seem to be spinning around you? Remember what you were *thinking* the last time you were upset, angry, or scared.

- What were you doing? What actions were you taking when this happened? Were you clenching your fists? Were you pacing the room? Remember the actions and *behaviors* you were engaging in the last time you were upset, angry, or scared.

Now that you remember what it's like when you are angry, upset, or scared, the next time you feel, think, or do any of those things you just listed, remind yourself to notice them and then stop.

Sometimes you'll forget to notice. In fact, when you start practicing enso politics, you'll forget a lot. You'll look back at an angry meeting where you yelled about how horrible that other activist is or recall how you couldn't stop wishing the other person in the room was stranded on an island. And later, when you realize that you got carried away, you'll promise yourself that next time (because there's always a next time), you will remember. And you might—or not. But the good news is that you'll remember sometimes. And when you do, then stop. Over time, you'll get better at noticing your own body's reactions to conflict or stress, and then you'll stop sooner and sooner until stopping becomes a reaction and you do it without even thinking.

Breathe

Now that you've stopped, take a minute to focus on your breathing. You can do this even while the rest of the room is spinning out of control, while your colleagues continue to yell, while chaos breaks out. Focusing on your breathing will calm you down physically and give you a chance to calm down mentally. This is guaranteed. As simple as the technique may sound, it makes a huge difference. Taking three good breaths usually does it.

A bunch of smart science reports document the power of breathing, but they are much too boring and long to quote, so I'll summarize them for you. Basically, when we humans get stressed or upset, our chest muscles contract, which causes us to breathe in shallower, shorter gulps. Those shallow, short breaths mean that we get less oxygen into our bodies, which means less oxygen to the brain, and our brains function best when they have lots of oxygen. The less oxygen moving to our brains, the more confused, irritable, sluggish, or tense we become. On the other hand, when we consciously choose to focus on our breathing and take deep, measured breaths (even as few as three), we restore critical amounts of oxygen to our brains and our bodies; we expel that nasty carbon dioxide from our bodies; and we increase our energy, calm our nerves, and reduce our feelings of stress.

That's a pretty good return on a small investment. And the great part is that you already know how to do this. You breathe all the time, and you can probably think of some recent times when you chose to stop and breathe in order not to do something drastic, like go crazy when the neighbor kid wrote in permanent marker all over your freshly painted living room wall.[3]

Watch

You stopped and you breathed. Now take one quick moment to watch. Take a look at what's going on—and look at the picture as if you were watching it from the outside, not as a player in the scene. The idea behind watching is to look at the situation from your new, relaxed perspective. Your head is clearer, you're calmer, and you've certainly got a different perspective than you did just five seconds ago. Now you can look at what's happening from a detached, emotionally unconnected place and just observe. What about this scenario is good? What about this is not good? What about it do you want to change? Just taking a moment to watch from an outside perspective can give you insight into what, if anything, you want to do next.

Decide to Do—or Don't Do

After you've watched the situation for a moment from a detached place of observation, you can make a decision about what to do next. You can go right back into the situation and choose to be upset or angry, you can leave the situation, you can change your feelings, whatever you choose. Or you can do nothing at all. What you actually do at this stage isn't important. What is important is that you're making a decision from a relaxed, comfortable place—a decision that isn't based on panic, fear, or anger.

• • •

Using these steps does not necessarily mean that your outward political behavior will change. I think that's pretty likely, but it's by no means an absolute. The key difference in your behavior will be this: you will consciously choose your behavior, whatever it may be, rather than unconsciously react to events as they arise. And that means that you control what you do and say in politics. When you are in control of what you do and say, you operate with a sense of centeredness. This makes you more confident and trustworthy and a better political activist.

I confess that I myself have trouble with enso politics. Even though I made up the term, introduced the concept in this chapter, and gave instructions on how to practice enso politics, I kind of stink at it. I practice it a lot, but it's very hard. I used to feel really bad and guilty about this until I read what the Dalai Lama said about meditating. You may know that Buddhist monks meditate for something along the lines of nineteen hours a day. One would expect all of them to be full of enlightenment, blissfully meditating to achieve nirvana every day. But the Dalai Lama said that they all stink at it too. This made me feel much better. Now I can practice enso politics and not feel bad if I sometimes stink at it because, hey—the Dalai Lama stinks at meditation.

To be quite honest, the person that I'm most likely to lose my cool with is none other than my best friend and colleague, Representative Chad Campbell. Chad and I have been friends for nearly a decade. When we met, Chad was doing some kind of computer IT genius job and was making good money. I told him that it'd be a great idea to help me run for office, even though he'd never managed a candidate campaign before and I was not the candidate slated to win. He agreed to help. Later, I told him that it'd be a good idea to quit his job and instead run a small nonprofit advocacy organization that I'd cofounded—for less than half the pay he was making at his real job. He agreed to do that. And later still, I roped him into running for the state legislature (under a secret theory that misery loves company). Chad has stuck with me through thick and thin, even when I made stupid mistakes and said stuff I shouldn't have said. He's a good friend.

But Chad has a temper. And although you can't tell by my smiling photo on the back of this book, so do I. Because we're as close as brother and sister, we've never had trouble treating each other as such. Like many siblings, we'd get into these little petty fights in person or on the phone. I can't even tell you what they were about—they were that stupid. But, oh, we'd go at it. Maybe we'd have an argument about a political tactic or something one of us had done at the capitol. You could hear us down the hall. During one altercation, Chad stormed out of my office and slammed the door so hard that the ugly photo on the wall outside my office fell down. (We laughed about that later, of course.) It was as if we were kids.

And then one day, something changed for me. I was on the phone arguing with Chad about something so dumb I can't remember it, and all of a sudden I stopped. It had just occurred to me that I was acting like a total moron, feeling angry and upset about something that wasn't really that big of a deal. And even if it had been a big deal, it wasn't worth yelling about. I took a deep breath, stayed quiet for a moment, and then said (very calmly), something to this effect: "This is crazy. I shouldn't be yelling about (whatever the issue was). I'm hanging up and we can talk about this later." Chad probably thought I had just had a stroke because I am not one to give up—over pretty much anything. But we hung up, and a few hours later the whole issue was resolved (whatever the heck it was). Since then, I've gotten better at practicing enso politics simply by taking that moment to stop and notice what's happening and what I'm feeling or thinking at the moment. I've found that I'm able to resolve problems faster, more smoothly, and more permanently. Putting down the bear and picking up the Buddha has made me a more effective political actor and a much happier person. It's also meant that other people want to work with me more, which is exactly what's needed to create coalitions for change.

Using Enso Politics in a Jiffy

Here's what to do when hanging onto the bear:

1. **Stop.** Notice that your head is about to explode and your ears are burning red with anger or frustration or humiliation or other strong emotion.

2. **Breathe.** Take three deep breaths, all nice and slow. Don't forget the breathing *in* part. (It's really important.) Now do the breathing *out* part. Good!

3. **Watch.** Pretend you're not part of the discussion or argument but that you're instead an invisible person watching from the sidelines.

4. **Do. Or don't do.** Make a decision about how to reenter the situation. Do you want to reengage? Leave? Change your words, posture, behavior? Make a decision and then do it. Or don't do anything.

Creating Coalitions You Actually Want to Join

Progressives love to talk about coalitions, but we're not very good at creating or maintaining them. In most cases, we get all the same ol' activists together in a room, and then one of two things happens: (1) whoever is in charge basically tells all the other people to forget their own interests and pony up for the "greater good," or (2) no one is in charge, and everyone sits around sniping at each other for months, never accomplishing a thing. Here, we'll explore what's wrong with our current coalition model and then establish a new model that actually gets progressives where we want to go.

Sometimes, we get into coalitions for coalitions' sake. Anytime there's a campaign, a problem to be addressed, or an issue to advance, everyone on the left says "get a broad-based coalition together!" We run out and ask our fifty progressive friends to join our coalition. They all say yes, so the same fifty-one people are members of yet another fancily named coalition of the moment. We then promptly forget about those coalition partners, except when we're doing a press release or need money. We've created a pseudo-coalition—it's for show, not for real. When progressives create pseudocoalitions over and over, we don't spend any real energy on creating deep, long-lasting relationships that lead to successful coalitions, and we're not able to marshal true coalition power to enact lasting change.

What can we do to create coalitions that are meaningful and useful and don't make us want to jump into the nearest well? The key ingredients that I think we need to start changing the way we think and act when building coalitions are new faces, purpose and focus, and leadership.

We Need New Faces

We're so busy in progressive politics. Most of us have the "yes" problem (I've got it in spades)—the one where we say yes to every single request that comes by. I find myself saying yes to the most ridiculous requests sometimes—to do tasks that are clearly not going to be the best use of my time and talents—because the people asking were just so nice. Anyway, we've got the "yes" problem, which leaves us overburdened and undertimed (I made that word up), and therefore usually in a frantic rush to do everything—including build coalitions.

I don't know anyone who gets paid to spend all of his or her time working on one coalition. The few people I know who are *supposed* to do coalition building for one group actually do that plus the work of two other staffers. It's the progressive way—overworked and underpaid.

"Right," you're thinking. "Tell me something I *don't* already live."

The point is you're so busy that it's crazy to think that you'd have a lot of extra time to build fabulous, effective, long-lasting coalitions. You do what you can in the time that you have, which generally means calling the standard group of folks who will always come when you call.

However, calling the folks you always call isn't enough in many, many instances. Most effective coalition work involves getting people to the table who don't already have a name-plate or a favorite chair. And that takes time and effort. So, what to do?

We need to take action to form meaningful relationships with people who are different from us, including really con-servative people. "Why on earth would I do that?" you may be thinking. Because you need those people to accomplish your goals. And they won't come running if you call now—they'll come only when they recognize your number (which they'll program into their cell phones only after you've become friends).

In the long run, you'll be able to put together a coalition of divergent people and groups on short notice and in short order. But you can get to that place only when you've made the connections with these folks and they trust you enough to come when you call. Start by making an effort to interact *now* with people who are different from you so that later, when it's time to form that oh-so-important coalition, you can easily collect those new faces around your coalition table.

The coalition "We Are America" in Arizona illustrates the im-portance of creating a broad-based coalition. Arizona, as you might know, is ground zero for the immigration crisis facing our country. The Minutemen (guys and gals who patrol the U.S.-Mexico border with guns searching for immi-grants crossing the border) founded their operation here and have flourished in the state.[1] Meanwhile, the immigrant population in Arizona continues to grow at the fastest rate in the country.[2] If there's a place in the country to talk about immigration, it's Arizona. We live it every day.

Back in March 2006, a group of activists organized a march in Phoenix to protest a bill in Congress (the Sensenbrenner bill) that would have reclassified undocumented immigrants as criminals and denied most of them an eventual path to citizenship, regardless of their length of residence in the United States, their work history, or their contribution to the country overall.[3] The gathering was much larger than anyone had anticipated—over twenty-five thousand people marched that day. Traffic was shut down, trash was left all over the street, and no one ordered portable toilets (which are *critical* to the success of any large event). It was a little bit of a logistical disaster, and the organizers were criticized in the media for days afterward. The day after the march, national news outlets reported that leaders in the immigration reform movement had declared April 10, 2006, a national day of action for sensible comprehensive immigration reform. This date was less than three weeks away, and we all knew that Arizona was going to have a march with a huge turnout.

Right about this time, some new people stepped up to the plate. Martin Manteca, who had recently moved to Arizona, came to my office and volunteered to help organize the next march. And, boy, can Martin organize—he'd organized in Chicago for years before moving to Arizona. In his short time in the state, he'd made connections with all types of folks and was clearly the right person to bring new people to this coalition. Cynthia Aragon, who worked with Martin, volunteered to help with the logistics, bookkeeping, and various other aspects of the event. Before a week had gone by, a whole new group of people had joined the effort to organize this march thanks to their outreach and organizing, from Latino activists to leaders in the African-American community, from faith leaders to civic engagement advocates, from Asian-Americans to college and high school student groups. We worked with state agencies, local governments, police departments, elected officials, community groups, and even the waste management folks to plan this massive march.

On April 10, 2006, over two hundred thousand people marched in Phoenix in support of comprehensive immigration reform.[4] According to my conversations with representatives of the Phoenix Police Department, the Arizona Capitol Police, and the Arizona Department of Public Safety, at the end of the day, not a scrap of garbage was left on the march route, not a single injury had occurred, no disturbances were reported, and no arrests were made.[5] The event was such a success, it brought together so many new faces, that the people involved created a lasting coalition, Somos America—We Are America. This group today includes a broad range of members—just as broad as when they started organizing for that march back in 2006. The coalition boasts leadership from those as young as twenty-two to veterans of the civil rights movement in the '50s and '60s. We Are America brought new faces to the table.

We Need Purpose and Focus

I love short-term projects. That might be why I have five part-time jobs instead of one real one, why I choose to serve in the legislature, and why I don't sew. What I love most about short-term projects is that each has a distinct beginning and end, with tasks to accomplish in the middle. The project has a purpose and a goal, and my job is to fulfill the purpose and achieve the goal. And before I get bored with the tediousness of the work, it's over.

On the other hand, coalitions that are formed for coalitions' sake and that last forever without focus or purpose make me want to tear my hair out. (Actually, I would rather tear out someone else's hair.) They have a saving grace: everyone knows each other, and often all the members are friends. They probably all trust each other. But regardless of who you are, these coalitions make everyone want to run away at some point. Over time, people will come up with more and more reasons they can't attend a coalition meeting, or staffers will assign a new, junior staff member to the coalition in order to get the meeting off their own calendar. And almost everyone will eventually leave the coalition—most members sooner rather than later.

How can we ensure that coalitions find that perfect balance between short-term, focused project and long-term relationship building? I think the answer lies in purpose and focus. When a coalition has a clearly articulated purpose (stop this bad legislation, win this ballot question, or influence this candidate's election) and is working in a focused way (with timelines, deliverables, assigned tasks, and accountability), people want to stay engaged and participate until the goal is reached. We should take care to clearly articulate the purpose of a given coalition and the focus of our respective work in it, even when the coalition consists of two or three people. After all, if you're not working in a focused and purposeful way, you're just friends hanging out. That's fun, but if you have a goal to achieve, hanging out isn't as useful as, say, working.

Even if a cause is compelling, a coalition can stagnate if it lacks a clear focus. For example, like all Americans, September 11th was a day I will never forget. I was driving to the Sunnyslope community of Phoenix that morning, thinking about my busy day ahead and idly listening to NPR in the background. When I heard the news about the first plane crash, I swerved so hard that I nearly hit a car in the next lane. Zombie-like, I pulled my car over to the side of the road and continued to listen to the coverage. After learning about the second plane crash, I began crying and couldn't stop. After a long while, I started my car again and drove the rest of the way to work. I knew that kids would need help that day, and my job as the social worker in the community was to provide that help. The day passed in a blur, with most of my time spent hugging kids and their parents and listening to people talk as they attempted to process what had just happened. Driving home that night, I called a friend and talked about what might happen next.

Within a few days, President Bush had made statements that I felt polarized our world and pushed away those who sought to join us in grieving.[6] As he began to talk about war,[7] a small group of Phoenicians began to organize. The group started meeting regularly, and we eventually formed a coalition called Arizona Alliance for Peaceful Justice. Our reason for existence was simple: to advocate for a diplomatic solution to the problems facing us and prevent, as much as possible, any war that would hurt civilians and the innocent. While we very strongly supported efforts to find and root out terrorism, we were worried that President Bush's movement to wage war in Iraq was unjustified, based on false information, and bad for our country and our world.

For several years, the coalition met regularly and planned and held marches, rallies, forums, and other events about the impending war. While the members of the coalition knew that war would happen regardless of our actions, we sought to raise awareness about the administration's false claims and the danger that this aggressive action would create for us around the globe. We accomplished some of our goals and garnered increased support from the community over the course of a few years. Once the United States actually launched the Iraq War, the coalition hit a plateau. Many people stopped participating in the group's activities, perhaps feeling that it wasn't useful to speak out against a war that had already started. Others likely saw the public's support of the war and decided to move on to other more fruitful work. (Remember in the early days of the Iraq War the public supported the intervention at rates of nearly 75 percent.) AAPJ meetings continued every two weeks, but they consisted of people discussing what they'd read in the national news or debating the finer points of foreign policy.

Events were small and attended by the same fifty people. The group spent little time engaging meaningfully with the public. AAPJ had trouble adapting its work to the new reality surrounding it. So I stopped attending and turned my attention to other projects I felt would be more productive. Many of my friends and colleagues did the same. The coalition had, for many of us, lost its purpose and its focus.

We Need Leadership

Coalitions are great because a bunch of people get to work together. And we progressives *love* to work collaboratively—except sometimes, when *collaborative work* is code for "We're floating on the open ocean and no one's steering the ship." That can be frustrating. Leadership is important in any coalition. It doesn't need to be despotic leadership (in fact, that's pretty passé), and it can be a leadership that shifts and changes over time, but leadership in some tangible form is almost always a prerequisite to a well-functioning coalition.

It's often said that if you put twelve progressives in a room, they'll come out with fourteen opinions. It's true that organizing a group of progressives is a bit like herding cats—it's frustrating and very difficult. Without strong leadership, it's impossible.

Smart coalitions involving more than three or four people establish leadership early on. Again, they often will make accommodations to share responsibilities and roles, but leadership is granted to someone in the group—to set meetings, call for accountability, and generally keep the ship moving forward. Without leadership, your coalition can quickly become stuck at sea, drifting around with no real direction. So assign a coalition member this role early on, and choose someone who is willing to hold others account-able, can manage a calendar, and isn't afraid to set meetings at 8:00 a.m.

In 2008, the Protect Arizona's Freedom coalition accom-plished great feats thanks to some strong, effective leader-ship. The coalition was formed in 2007 after a few of us in Arizona learned that Ward Connerly was planning to bring his anti–equal opportunity initiative to our state. Connerly is a California businessman who once served on the board of regents for that state's university system. While on the board, Connerly began speaking out against college and university programs that provided specific assistance to female stu-dents and students of color. He also wanted to stop the state's practice of providing dedicated small business con-tracts to women- and minority-owned businesses, which had been instituted to help these historically marginalized populations get a foot in the door of business, so to speak. (I've always been puzzled by why Connerly wanted to end this practice, especially because he got his start in business through some of these very contracts.) He began working in California to change state law to prevent women and minor-ities from having access to dedicated educational programs and to eliminate small business contracts for women and minorities. He successfully passed a ballot initiative in California in 1996 to make these changes and then went on to pass similar initiatives in Washington (1998) and Michigan

(2006). In 2007, he announced his intention to bring the initiative to eleven more states, including Arizona.

One morning around the middle of 2007, I was sitting in my office at the state capitol and saw none other than Ward Connerly standing in the Rose Garden downstairs, flanked by reporters. I called Chad in his office and we raced downstairs to see what Connerly was up to. Turns out, he was announcing his intention to launch a ballot initiative in Arizona to prohibit our colleges and universities from offering programs for women and students of color to ensure their success. Now I don't like it when a rich guy from California swoops into my state and says he's going to change our laws. He can change his own state's laws all he wants, but only Arizonans should change Arizona's laws. And frankly, I think our laws concerning college programs are just fine. We like to encourage women to study science, math, and engineering, and we like providing programs to help Native American students stay in college and graduate.

A group of educators, activists, elected officials, and community members started meeting every two weeks to plan how we were going to stop Connerly. We met for months on end, made grand plans, and accomplished a few goals. We did some polling on the issue and learned about Connerly's efforts to take his campaign to other states and change their laws too. Finally, Connerly started the process of gathering signatures in Arizona to qualify his initiative for the ballot. In our state, any individual can put a proposed change to the law on the state ballot if he or she collects about 330,000 signatures from registered voters and turns them in to the state by early July. This is no easy task—it usually costs about a half million dollars to get an initiative on the ballot, and it takes months for the people hired to collect signatures to actually get them.

By spring 2008, we'd heard about Connerly's troubles in other states, such as Oklahoma and Missouri, where he failed to gather enough signatures. Some people in our coalition wondered whether he'd gather enough valid signatures to put his initiative on the Arizona ballot. I believed that if we decided to just wait and see, we wouldn't have the time or the person power to challenge the validity of the signatures. Plus, Connerly had declared Arizona as his most important state for the 2008 election cycle, I knew he wouldn't give up without a fight. Rather than waiting, we decided to act.

Based on court records from Michigan (where Connerly launched and passed his initiative in 2006) and news reports about Missouri and Oklahoma (where his initiative failed to qualify for the ballot on 2008), I believed that Connerly routinely hired a pretty shady signature-gathering firm based in Florida to run his signature campaigns.[8] This firm has a history of engaging in fraudulent behavior, as noted in Oklahoma in 2006 (three employees were indicted for identity theft) and rumored in other states.[9] Arizona law says that only state residents who have the legal right to vote can collect signatures from other voters. Clearly, it's illegal for a firm from Florida to bring people into our state to collect signatures. I also had read reports from Colorado (where Connerly was also operating in 2008) disclosing the fact that Connerly's folks weren't doing background checks on the people they hired to make sure they were qualified to circulate peti-tions. And finally, we knew that Connerly had started gath-ering signatures fairly late in the season and so would be pressed for time to gather all 330,000-plus signatures. When paid circulators are in a hurry, they tend to make lots of mis-takes and sometimes cut corners—like, for instance, copy-ing people's names out of phone books (which is illegal), list-ing Robert and John Kennedy as Arizona voters even though they're dead, and my personal favorite, signing up Muam-mar al-Kaddafi (president of Libya).[10]

We had ample evidence that funny stuff would likely be happening with the signatures, and we were determined to monitor them and file suit in court, if necessary, to stop the initiative from qualifying for the ballot if had Connerly used the same fraudulent tactics in Arizona that he'd used in other states.

Successfully challenging the validity of initiative signatures in Arizona is very hard because you have only two and a half weeks in which to review all the signatures, identify all legal infirmities, put together a legal claim, and file and resolve the lawsuit. People are often successful on smaller issues such as candidate challenges, city initiatives, and the like. It's possible to handle those types of cases because you're responsible for only several hundred to twenty thousand signatures or so, which is totally manageable in a three-week time period. But 330,000 signatures in eighteen days? Sounds impossible.

But not for us. I gathered a group of volunteer attorneys to help me with the legal research, worked with a local law firm, connected with national partners to get advice and help, and convinced Cynthia Aragon to become the lead organizer of the project, which we called Protect Arizona's Freedom.

Cynthia is a born organizer. She can organize anything. When she became the lead organizer for Protect Arizona's Freedom, I knew we were going to win. In the one month we spent preparing for our eighteen-day signature-checking marathon, Cynthia managed to bring together nearly one thousand volunteers from around the state, scheduled them for round-the-clock shifts, and worked with local community organizations to ensure broad support for our project.

During the eighteen days, Cynthia and I practically lived at the PAF office. She was there when the sun came up in the morning and left close to midnight each night (while our night crew continued to work!). Her responsibility for the project was immense: ensure that we had the right number of volunteers each shift, train people for each task, transition from task to task without mistakes, and keep the entire train running on time. Cynthia was a machine. Throughout those eighteen days, volunteers knew that she was in charge of their part of the operation, and they knew that she'd keep things rolling. When problems or unexpected occurrences arose, Cynthia adapted. The entire coalition worked effectively over the course of those eighteen days because we'd chosen a leader who wasn't afraid to keep the coalition moving forward at all times.

• • •

It's not always enough just to invite new people, articulate a purpose and focus, and support good leadership, but without those three things, your coalition can't work. In the rest of this book, we'll cover other vital ingredients of a working, effective coalition. But don't forget to bring these three tools with you.

BONUS BOX

Recipe for a Coalition

These three vital ingredients are needed for building a successful, productive coalition.

1. **Think big.** Include people who aren't already at the table. Who are unlikely allies or potential partners in your project? Whom can you bring to the table that will surprise you and those around you?

2. **Think sharp.** Clearly articulate your purpose and your focus. What is your coalition's raison d'être? If you don't know, then your coalition isn't likely to be effective.

3. **Think organized.** Choose a leader (stable or rotating) who will keep the coalition organized and productive. Don't leave anything to chance because chance is not your friend.

4

Shedding the Heavy Mantle of Victimhood

One of the greatest obstacles to creating effective coalitions is our obsession with victimhood. Progressives make great victims. We've had a lot of practice at it. We are used to being picked on, marginalized, ignored, and hated. As a result, we developed the phenomenon often referred to as *identity politics*. The idea behind identity politics boils down to this: "I am different from you in some fundamental respect and therefore need my own group that understands me. And also, I can't work with you." This is a useful strategy to employ when you're being physically attacked because the small group can band together and only the people on the outer ring of the circle get hit by the rocks thrown by the attackers. Many of us who are members of a historically marginalized group (women, people of color, lesbian and gay people, people with disabilities, and more) know what it's like to have rocks thrown at us, so we instinctively stay in those small circles *just in case* more rocks are coming our way.

However, if your goal is to achieve some sort of political change that results in more rights or protections or benefits for your group, then identity politics is not useful at all. Because each "identity group" is necessarily made up of a small (and historically politically disenfranchised) group, the group is, by definition, *small*. Small doesn't win elections. In fact, small pretty much always loses. It's easy to understand why: when your group comprises 3 to 4 percent or even

15 percent of the electorate, you lose when you work alone. Three percent is nowhere near 50 percent plus one.

Rejecting Identity Politics

Rejecting identity politics isn't easy to do, but the results can be transformative. Here's an example of what can happen when you move beyond identity politics. Airick Leonard West is a twenty-eight-year-old college dropout. He's African-American and was raised by a white foster family in southern Missouri, the most conservative part of a state not exactly known for its progressivism. He has seen and experienced identity politics his whole life.

When Airick discovered a latent talent for computers, he went to work in the dot-com industry, making money hand over fist. But the dot-com world didn't quite work for Airick. He says, "Somewhere in the back of my mind, I thought if I could be successful in the dot-com industry, if I made enough money, then I would be accepted there as who I was: a bright guy with a successful company making lots of money. Turns out, that was not the case. I was still just some black kid."[1] This was a call to reality for Airick. He moved to Kansas City, Missouri, began working part-time at night to pay the bills, and devoted his life to building a community dedicated to the kids of Kansas City.

Somewhere along the way he was persuaded to run for public office. Today, Airick is the newest member of the Kansas City Missouri School District, elected to the at-large seat in the spring of 2008. Almost ten years ago, state officials stripped the school district of its accreditation, and in the fall of 2007 the superintendent was booted after just eighteen months on the job. People in Kansas City generally understand that you don't send your kids to a KCSMD school unless they have nowhere else to go. Yet Airick left a lucrative dot-com career to run for an unpaid school board seat in a loser district. Why? Because he believes in unity.

It's the cornerstone of his campaign, his community work, and his philosophy of life: "The concept of unity is not just a random abstraction. It's a sense that we can find common cause. The reality is that when we come together around a common vision, there will be compromise. The edges of our individual visions may be trimmed in lieu of the larger collective vision. And so unity, while a powerful force for transformation in the community, is not without a measure of sacrifice from the people involved."[2] Airick believes that for years, people have been content to live within the stratified compounds of race or class or what have you—the *silos* as he calls them—without working together. But this type of identity politics hasn't produced the results we need for our community, and that's what Airick can't stand.

Airick's work is all about rejecting identity politics, pulling people out of their silos—their self-imposed separatist groupings based on race, class, gender, sexual orientation, and so on—and getting people to work together for a larger common goal. Here is an excerpt from his campaign Web site:

> Unity is not everyone agreeing. This campaign is
> joined by many people who don't often agree with

each other. But we do agree that educational achievement is a journey worth pursuing . . .

Unity is not the absence of diversity. We invite all people—district residents, non-residents, citizens, non citizens, people of color, people not of color, youth, seniors and so forth—to stand with us. And our kind of unity asks no one to leave their individuality behind. Rather, we simply acknowledge that we are all part of the greater whole that is necessary to create educational achievement for our students.[3]

It's no wonder that he won his seat.

Airick could have done things differently. He could have run for the District 3 seat for the school board, which would have been easier to win. Instead, he ran for a district-wide seat against an incumbent who was poised to be president of the school board. When asked why he chose the harder route, Airick's answer was simple: unity. Airick wanted to bring people together more than he wanted to win the easy way. For him, it's all about eschewing identity politics and embracing a larger concept of unity.

His governance style rejects identity politics as well. He's served on the school board for under a year, but his actions are already living up to his reputation. He rejects attempts to classify the students in his school district as poor, underperforming kids because of their race or income, instead focusing on the need for resources, training, and effective teaching. He has converted even admitted skeptics, and the school district is moving toward reaccreditation and a stable leadership team at district headquarters. As he told the *New York Times* in March 2008, "Unity isn't this kumbaya illusion. To take on the status quo, you need to transcend a single group."[4]

Airick could have chosen the path of least resistance. He probably would have been elected to the same school board from his local district. He could have chosen to serve on that board as a voice solely for the African-American community. He probably would have gotten some great kudos from his neighbors for it. In fact, Airick probably could have been a moderately successful politician for years to come if he had clung to identity politics. But by consciously choosing to re-ject identity politics, to align himself with African-Americans, Latinos, Anglos, business leaders, school administrators, teachers, students, and community leaders, he created a very broad coalition, which will create limitless capacity for change and transformation in his community. And Airick himself can continue in politics—running for and winning future offices in Missouri—because he's consciously chosen to nudge people out of their silos and into a broader concept of unity.

Identity Politics Gone Wild

In the 2004 elections, seventeen states across the country passed constitutional amendments to ban same-sex mar-riage, by way of popular vote. (Many states have an initiative process, where people can put proposed changes to the law or constitution directly to the people for a vote.) Arizona didn't have such a marriage initiative on the ballot in 2004, which was a little surprising, considering that Arizona is a very initiative-friendly state. With half a million dollars and at least four months of time, you can put anything up for a vote. So when the dark days of November 2004 had passed (boy, that was a depressing election night), we here in Arizona started looking around and wondering why we hadn't faced a marriage ban. Turns out that the religious right was saving Arizona for 2006. Our popular governor, Janet Napolitano, was up for reelection in 2006, and some on the political right deemed a marriage initiative as just the thing to counter her popularity and bring out voters who would support the ban and vote to defeat her.

A small group of us met in January 2005 to prepare for the initiative battle. We began by conducting research, which showed that the initiative could be defeated in the state but that it wouldn't be easy or cheap. As we considered our options and prepared to meet with activists around the state to decide what to do, I found myself drafted as the chair of the coalition.

In May 2005, we'd toured the state, met with allied people and groups, and formed an official coalition—Arizona Together. (I discuss this process more in chapter 11.) Arizona Together was formed with one major goal in mind: earning more no votes on Proposition 107 than the proponents earned yes votes. We knew that it wouldn't be easy to earn more votes than the other side (after all, it had never been done), so we carefully considered what it would take to win. We focused on crafting a winning message, utilizing trained messengers, and raising adequate money to get our message across to the voters. After spending thousands of dollars on research, we crafted a message that our research indicated would resonate with a majority of Arizona voters. We formed a broad-based coalition that reached well beyond the traditional allied community and garnered support from unlikely people and groups. (I write more about this in chapter 8.) And we raised as much money as we could in order to spread our message across the state.

Our campaign message was unique (as was most of the campaign, really). We focused on the impact that the initiative would have on unmarried couples in the state, rather than fighting with the proponents about the merits of same-sex marriage. This was a significant decision for us. Because same-sex marriage has been prohibited by state law since 1996, we didn't see any value in arguing over that part of the initiative, which wouldn't have an immediate impact on people's lives. That part was intended to appeal emotionally to voters, not to change anything about daily life in our state. But a major part of the initiative would immediate impact Arizonans on day one of its passage: the amendment would prohibit any legal recognition of domestic partnerships in Arizona. The state and most local governments provide domestic health benefits for unmarried employees, their partners, and their children, and this initiative would take those health-care benefits away from the employees' partners and their kids. It also would prohibit unmarried seniors from visiting each other in the hospital and prevent unmarried couples from making medical decisions for each other.

Lots of people were surprised when they learned this. After all, this initiative was called a "same-sex marriage ban." How come it didn't actually change anything in Arizona about same-sex marriage and instead sought to take away protections and benefits of unmarried couples, both straight and gay? Marketing. The proponents knew that they needed to focus on the marriage part of the proposition because Arizona voters are conflicted on the issue of marriage for gay people (as are most voters throughout the country). Arizona voters are pretty firmly set in their support for domestic partnership recognition, though, so ignoring this part of the proposition was important to its proponents. We knew that the opposition needed to focus on what regular Arizonans would *lose* if the initiative passed—the protections and benefits that exist for unmarried couples statewide. So our media effort talked about one unmarried couple in particular—Al and Maxine.

Al and Maxine are an elderly retired couple who live in Tucson. They can't get married because Maxine would lose her first husband's pension payments and they'd be too poor to take care of themselves. That's why they have lived together for years without getting married. A few years ago, Maxine got really ill and was in the intensive care unit. Because Tucson recognizes domestic partners, Al was able to sit by her side during her entire illness. But if Proposition 107 passed, Al would be legally prohibited from going into the ICU to see Maxine.

This is a great little story, isn't it? Just writing it, I get upset and worried for Al and Maxine all over again. Of course they should get to be with each other in the hospital! Well, the voters agreed, as we figured they would, and the proposition was defeated. By all accounts, it was an incredibly successful campaign—the first campaign in the nation to defeat a proposed same-sex marriage ban! Arizona is usually near the top of the list in stuff like teen birth rate and high school dropout rate and auto theft rate, but never are we first in something good, so we felt pretty proud of this election.

However, not everyone felt proud, either during or after the campaign. I still get angry e-mails from some members of the LGBT community. At first, this really surprised me. I mean, this was a historic victory! I would think people would send flowers—or chocolates (I really like chocolate). But no. Turns out, a whole lot of people didn't like this campaign because they felt it didn't speak enough to the trials and tribulations of the LGBT community (which most certainly exist in Arizona). Because the campaign told the story of Al and Maxine, a *straight* couple who would be hurt by the passage of the initiative, a number of people accused me and the rest of our team of "throwing the gay community under the bus."[5]

I was surprised by the reaction—until I remembered identity politics. Because the crux of identity politics is the *separateness* of one small group from the larger community, people who believed in identity politics saw the Arizona Together campaign as denying that separateness and pushing all the gay and straight people together into one big lump. When I figured this out, I said, "Yes! That's exactly it! We are all in this together! We're one big lump! That's why we're called Arizona Together! We're together. *All together! Get it?"*

They did not get it. What they got instead was a strong feeling of denial—a denial of their own uniqueness and validity. During the campaign they said to me, "We should not talk about Al and Maxine; we should talk about how the people proposing this initiative are bigots and hateful people." They said, "Why are we talking about straight people in this campaign? It's really about the right-wingers who hate the gays." They said, "We should tell the voters not to write discrimination into the constitution against gay people." I said, "Umm—no. The point here is that this is *not* about you. It is about us and our state and all of us together. All of Arizona will be affected if this initiative passes, not just one identity group. And yes, gay and lesbian people will be grievously hurt. And so will lots of straight people. Because we're all in this together."

You see, a bunch of other states around the country had already passed this very initiative. In those states, some of the groups opposed to the initiatives had said, "Don't discriminate against one group of people" and "Don't let the bigots rain their hate down upon the gays" and "Stop being mean to gay people because they're just as good as you." And that's all identity politics language. It's all about one group, to the exclusion of everyone else. When we cling to identity politics, we shut out people who are different from us in one or more fundamental ways but who are *like us* in other ways. In Arizona, we knew that everyone understood the importance of health care and hospital visitation rights, no matter their sexual orientation. We also knew that many people in the state were struggling, like so many other Americans are, with the concept of gay people and gay families and gay relationships. Far be it from me to tell them their struggle is wrong or bad. We all have our own struggles, and we're all doing our best to deal with them. In the Arizona Together campaign, we decided that it was okay for people to have struggles (to decide otherwise would have been futile, of course) but that their struggles didn't need to get in the way of defeating this initiative. In other words, we wanted to create a situation where a voter who was conflicted about relationship recognition for gay people could vote no on Proposition 107 and feel comfortable with that vote. And so we dropped identity politics in favor of the largest circle we could draw—the whole state.

• • •

Ditching identity politics can be scary. But when progressives decide to view those around them not as enemies from a different tribe but instead as potential allies who can come together for a larger purpose, great coalitions can be formed—so great, in fact, that you wonder why you ever bought into identity politics in the first place.

BONUS BOX

The Cure to the Dread Disease of Identity Politics

Here are some ways we can get past identity politics and work together:

1. **Get over yourself.** This is a hard step, because none of us really want to get over ourselves. But if you spend all your time attached to yourself and are unable to broaden your worldview to include others, you will always lose.

2. **Dump the silos.** The civil rights movement of the '50s and '60s involved African-Americans, Anglos, Latinos, faith leaders, secular leaders, attorneys, students, radicals, conservatives, and more. If we could get past our silos then, we can do it now.

3. **Open up.** Think about the cause or issue you care about most. Now think about who else might care about it— *even if the people don't seem likely or obvious*. Now go find those people and invite them to work with you or your shared cause or issue.

5

Making Friends

In the middle of the 2008 campaign season, I called a meeting of lobbyists, activists, and representatives from various groups to see if they were interested in forming a coordinated "No on Everything" campaign. Arizona had eight initiatives on the ballot, and they were all stinkers. Some were just plain stupid, others were repeats of bad ideas from prior years, and a few were flat-out dangerous. I'd been hearing people talk about how Arizonans should just vote no on everything, and I wondered if there was some real energy around the idea. I called a bunch of people who I knew were working on the various "No" campaigns, and I asked them to attend the meeting. Pretty much everyone I called came, including a couple of very conservative Republican lobbyists and politicos. You should have seen the looks on my liberal activist friends' faces when they saw each of these guys walk into the meeting and take a seat. I could feel their gaze slide from the conservative guy's tie over to my face, with a quiet look that said "What the heck are you doing, Sinema?" I just smiled at everyone and began introductions around the room.

We had a very productive meeting and began working on the coordinated strategy. What brought us together was neither conservative nor liberal, Republican nor Democrat—it was finding a way to win. Once the progressive folks in the room got over their shock and distrust about the conservatives in the room, we were able to have a good conversation about what we all shared in common that election season and how we could work together to achieve our goal.

After the meeting, I got a call from one of the more liberal members at the meeting, a representative of the animal rights community. She talked for a moment about the strategy we were working on, expressed her hope and optimism about the concept, and said to me, "You sure do have a talent for bringing together some interesting coalitions." I couldn't quite tell if she meant it as a compliment or not. But it certainly is a reflection of one of my earliest and best-learned lessons in politics: make friends with the other guys.

As I mentioned, I had a hard time making friends my first year in the legislature. People were mostly polite to me and complimented my outfits, but no one wanted to actually *work* with me. At first, I blamed my situation on the politics of division that my Republican colleagues had been taught. But I soon realized that the blame was largely mine. I also had been taught the politics of division—namely, that my role as a minority member in the house of representatives was to stand and loudly speak out against the horrible, evil injustices committed daily by my Republican peers. Somehow, I thought they'd realize the error of their ways, become my friends, and then help me pass all my bills. Shockingly, I was wrong. I learned that dividing myself from others just because we don't agree on everything is *not* the way to win friends and influence people. I threw out what I'd been taught and started over—this time remembering what my kindergarten teacher told me: make friends with the other kids. Here are the tips that I've found helpful when making friends: (1) talk to the people whom you want to make friends with, (2) listen to them, (3) find common ground, (4) find humanity in others, (5) loosen up a bit, and (6) don't take anything personally.

Talk to Them

The very first step to making friends is pretty simple. Talk to them. It sounds so easy, doesn't it? Sometimes it is. Most times, though, it's not quite as easy as it sounds. You may have to wade through disapproval from your friends and fellow activists. You may have to shock onlookers as you walk across the room at a political event toward the huddle of conservatives standing far, far away from the bar. But it's worth it. If you don't make the first step toward that person who is different from you, the step will likely never be made by anyone.

No one has done this quite as well as Ken Cheuvront, my state senator. Ken is the first openly gay man ever elected to public office in Arizona. Ken owns a wine and cheese bar in central Phoenix and, while fiscally conservative, is quite socially liberal. He became a state representative in 1994, and in 1996, a highly conservative woman named Karen Johnson was elected to the state legislature. Karen is a devout Mormon from the east valley (a bastion of uber-conservative thought in Arizona). In her first years in the legislature, she gave speeches stating that gay men were "on the lower end of the behavioral spectrum."[1] She introduced a bill to make sodomy a felony and tried to outlaw gay-tolerance groups from high school campuses. She doesn't believe in alcohol consumption, is 100 percent antichoice, and loves guns. Clearly, Ken and Karen were worlds apart.

Several years ago, Karen and Ken were both elected to the state senate and the senate president seated them next to each other on the floor. They talked each day on the floor, and over the years they were able to close part of the political gap between them. The two became friends—close friends, in fact. Many saw them talking to each other every day, smiling and laughing and sharing stories. But few realized just what a difference their seating arrangement made—until June 2008. Karen announced early in 2008 that she was retiring from the legislature after the current session. She still introduced legislation to allow adults to bring guns onto campuses—including elementary school campuses—and legislation calling for an investigation into 9/11, which she believes was a conspiracy.[2] But her friendship with Ken changed her views in one area in particular. Karen, who used to give speeches comparing gay relationships to bestiality, was opposed to the legislative referendum to ban same-sex marriage in 2008. Karen eventually voted yes in response to her constituents' views on the issue, but she told the Arizona Republic after the vote, "I wish I had a little more courage." She explained her opposition to the measure in part by saying, "Ken lives and lets live, and I feel that's probably where I should be, too."[3]

Ken and Karen became close friends at the capitol, despite their very different worldviews and experiences, and despite all political odds. Their friendship changed the way they thought about each other and even the way they thought about some things in the world. And it all started because they talked to each other.

Listen to Them

Listening to others is key. Progressives are often much better at talking than listening, but listening matters. People want to feel heard and they want to be understood. Listening to those who aren't already on your side or in your pocket is a great way to learn about who they really are, what they really care about, and what they think should be done to solve problems that we face. You may not agree with all (or any) of what a new friend says, but listening will help you gain insight into that person's world-view and understand who he or she really is. And listening without interrupting and arguing with your friend about how global warming is real will help even more. When people are allowed to talk about their views and beliefs without interruption, provocation, or argument, they're much more likely to be honest and genuine. Honesty and genuineness are so rare in politics that I believe we should treasure them when we find them. Even if the speaker's honest and genuine beliefs are anathema to you, it's valuable to know them.

I'm not very good at this step. I get so wrapped up in the issue under discussion that I desperately want to insert my two cents—or more often, my two hundred cents. In the moment of discussion, I convince myself that if I can just state my case and my facts clearly, the other person can't fail to agree with me. As you can imagine, this goes over like gangbusters. Instead of listening to the other person's beliefs, I find myself in a debate, which does absolutely nothing to forge friendships. Later, I may kick myself for jumping from listening to debating, but by then it's too late.

Luckily, some people are really, really good at this, so I'll tell one of their stories instead. Bill Richardson is serving his second term as a wildly popular governor of New Mexico. Prior to running for governor, he served in Congress for fourteen years, as a United Nations ambassador for two years, and as the United States energy secretary for three years. That's a pretty impressive resume. But then add to that his nominations for the Nobel Peace Prize—he has earned five. Clearly he's doing something right in the area of making friends. Richardson himself credits his ability to forge relationships with even the worst dictators in the world on his willingness to listen.[4]

Over the course of a twenty-five-year career in politics and diplomacy, Richardson has negotiated the release of hostages, prisoners, and soldiers in Cuba, Iraq, North Korea, and Sudan. In 1994, he traveled to North Korea to secure the release of an American Army pilot, then went back in 1996 to rescue another American hostage. In 1995, he traveled to Baghdad and engaged in lengthy negotiations with Saddam Hussein to garner the release of two American aerospace workers who accidentally walked past the Kuwaiti border into Iraq. In 2006, during the (continuing) genocide in Darfur at the hands of the Sudanese government, Richardson was called from his duties as a western state governor to Sudan in order to meet with Sudanese president Omar al-Bashir to negotiate the release of Paul Salopek, an American reporter, and his two Sudanese translators. In just thirty minutes of conversation with the Sudanese president—thirty minutes in which the president did most of the talking—Richardson secured the release of the three prisoners. And in 2007, Richardson traveled to North Korea to negotiate the release of the remains of six American soldiers, all of whom were killed during the Korean War.[5] For years, the American government has sought the remains of thousands of American soldiers who died during the Korean War, but only rarely have we been able to recover any of those remains. Each of these extraordinary trips, and their extraordinary results, come from Bill Richardson's willingness to listen to those who are different from himself.

My favorite example of Governor Richardson's uncanny ability to listen to others occurred during his 1996 trip to Sudan. As a congressman from New Mexico, Richardson successfully negotiated the release of three Red Cross workers held hostage by Sudanese rebels—just two weeks after successfully negotiating the release of an American held hostage in North Korea. He'd been asked to travel to Sudan by the wife of one of the hostages (a New Mexican), the International Red Cross, and the government of Sudan. He flew to the rebel outpost and met with the leader, a tough and unpredictable man named Kerubino Kwanyin Bol. Kerubino began the meeting by demanding $2.5 million in exchange for the hostages, which of course Richardson could not agree to.

Instead, Richardson listened as Kerubino complained about the effect that the United States' embargo on Sudan was having on the rural communities in the country. Children were dying of cholera and dysentery, and Kerubino's own two year-old daughter had died two days earlier from measles. After hours of listening to Kerubino's litany of concerns, Richardson told Kerubino that it sounded like the rebels needed help with humanitarian issues such as medical attention and food. Turns out, this is exactly what Kerubino wanted (even though he hadn't asked for it in his original demand). In the end, Kerubino agreed to release the hostages in exchange for vaccines, food, and sanitization of the local water source for the southern Sudan rebels and their community. By listening to what was really bothering the Sudanese rebels, Richardson was able to get the community what it needed and return home with the Red Cross workers.[6]

Does Bill Richardson agree with the political views and tactics of these and other rogue leaders around the globe? Absolutely not. But, as *Time* magazine said about him in 1996, he has a "knack for finding a warm spot in even the surliest of despots."[7] By listening to the people he's negotiating with, Richardson learns what they really want or need from a given situation and then finds a way to meet that need. It's an incredible gift, and few of us will ever be as good at listening as Bill Richardson is. But his example provides a lesson for us all: listen to hear what the other person really cares about and really wants.

Find Common Ground

Sometimes when you're reaching across the proverbial aisle, you wonder what you're going to take hold of on the other side. Part of making friends is finding some common ground. It doesn't have to be a lot of ground—any little patch will do. But find something that brings you closer to the other person, and then spend a little time talking about that commonality. I conduct a citizen lobbying training in Arizona that teaches regular Arizonans how to come to the capitol and influence policy. One of the first actions that I recommend to people is to learn about their legislator *before* scheduling a meeting at the capitol with him or her. Find out the legislator's likes and interests, learn about his or her family, figure out where the legislator went to school or what church he or she attends. Knowing this kind of information will always lead to some common ground. Maybe you both have children around the same age—you'll always find plenty of common ground when teenagers are concerned. Perhaps your sister or cousin attended the same high school or college as the legislator. Whatever it is, there will always be some common ground. You can use this point of commonality as a starting place for your relationship. People, even rabidly political people, like to talk about something other than politics once in a while. Starting a conversation with something "normal" like your common ground can make both people in the conversation feel more comfortable and trusting.

Here's another Bill Richardson story, this time about finding common ground. When Richardson traveled to Cuba in 1996 to negotiate with Fidel Castro about the release of three American hostages, he started the conversation with baseball. Richardson's mother is from Mexico and he spent most of his childhood in Mexico, playing baseball religiously. He later played professionally in the United States before entering politics. He knew about Castro's love of baseball and studied up on Castro's personality and style, so when he arrived to meet with Castro, Richardson spoke in Spanish and started the several-hour meeting by talking about what they had in common—a love of baseball. In the end, Richardson left Cuba with three freed hostages.[8]

Finding common ground won't lead most of us to a life of freeing hostages from hostile dictators, but it always makes for a great foundation in one's quest to make friends and form lasting relationships. I made friends with one Republican lobbyist years ago over a couple of laughs. He'd asked to meet in late 2004, right after I'd been elected but before my first session started. He lobbies for the construction industry, and I'm a pretty solid partner for the environmental community, so we didn't have a whole lot in common policywise. In fact, his organization had nearly decided to spend money attacking my views in the 2004 election due to its members' concern about my positions on environmental issues. Not an auspicious beginning, most would concur. But I agreed to meet him at a coffee shop by my house anyway, and we talked for about an hour. I don't think we agreed on a single policy issue that day. But he had a great sense of humor, and once we agreed that I'd vote against most of his bills in the upcoming session and that he'd work hard to kill all of my bills, we just had fun joking around about the elections and political life. I knew we'd get along pretty well when, upon leaving the coffee shop and walking to the parking lot, I immediately identified his car as the one with the big camouflage "Sportsmen for Bush" sticker on it. As I laughed about his sticker, he pointed to the rainbow "Kerry-Edwards" sticker nearby on my little hybrid and joked right back. Today, we still disagree on most policy issues, but we've got a great record of working together on issues in which we can find a reasonable compromise. And when we can't come to an agreement on a specific issue, we can at least always share a laugh.

Find Humanity

After I started making friends at the capitol, life got a lot easier for me. I could chat with Republican legislators in the hallway, joke with a right-wing lobbyist before a floor session, and laugh with a wild-eyed liberal on the floor. But I was still having trouble with Russell Pearce. Russell is quite a guy. He's a legislator from east Mesa, and he's got an issue about immigration. Actually, pretty much all Russell cares about is immigration. Once in a while, he'll stop railing about so-called illegals to advocate reducing health care funding for children or lifesaving treatment for pregnant women, but he's mostly about immigration. As a former social worker in an immigrant and refugee community, I care about immigration too. My views are a tad different from Russell's, though (as you can probably tell), so making friends with Russell was not an easy task. He kept doing and saying things that I felt made it even harder for me to make friends with him. In a 2006 radio interview he stated that he wanted to reinstate Operation Wetback, a 1953 federal program that sought to round up and deport all undocumented workers in the country. Not only was this a bad idea, he actually *said* the word "wetback" on the air! Later, when called upon to apologize by various communities throughout the state, he refused, stating that he liked to use "very graphic" terms to make his point.[9]

This was a tough one for me. Several months afterward, I was still hurting from the *w* word. So when Russell and I were invited to debate each other on the issue of immigration for a local television program, I knew I needed to prepare for the debate. I'd avoided him pretty much since that comment—and because we don't serve on any committees together, it hadn't been much of a problem. But I didn't want to get angry at him or blow up on television. We showed up at the studio to tape the program and waited in the green room for close to half an hour. (The green room experience is always an interesting one. I think the television people put us all in there with a secret camera just to see what we'll do and say.) I set about my self-appointed task for the evening: to make friends with Russell Pearce. It wasn't easy going because even during small talk, Russell can manage to squeeze in some anti-immigrant comments that rankle my soul, but I was determined. After a while, someone in the room asked him about his plans for the weekend. He began talking about his favorite thing to do: take his wife to the movies. I think he even said "picture show." They go almost every weekend and share a popcorn and M&M's. I can't remember all the details, but I do remember this: I looked at Russell and said to myself suddenly, "That man loves his wife. He may not believe in the same kind of protections for women who are victims of domestic violence that I do, and he may think that the state shouldn't spend money on kids with disabilities, but he loves his wife." And in that moment I saw humanity in Russell Pearce.

We went into the studio a few minutes later and held our debate. Sometimes he made outrageous statements that I could hardly believe. But through it all, it was easier than I'd expected to debate calmly because I remembered that Russell loves his wife. And from then on, I found it easier to talk with Russell about almost anything. We've even been able to work together on a few items at the capitol. Russell supported my Sudan legislation (I talk about this bill in chapter 10), and we worked together several years ago to pass legislation establishing a monument to the Bill of Rights on our state capitol grounds.

Russell and I still disagree on almost everything, but I no longer feel as hot in the head when he's talking about opinions or policies I disagree with because I can remember how his voice sounded and how his face looked when he talked about taking his wife to the picture show. And because I remember that, I can more often approach him from a place of friendship instead of antagonism.

Loosen Up

When I first got to the capitol, I'd get so mad when colleagues stood up and gave moralizing speeches about issues like abortion, child care, and a myriad of other social issues. My blood would start to boil, and I'd fume for hours. The wheels in my head would turn so fast that I felt hot, and rolling around and around in my head were thoughts like "Who does so-and-so think he is? Talk about pulling yourself up by the bootstraps—these kids don't even have boots!" After the floor session ended, I'd stomp up to my office, furious about whatever major injustice had just occurred. Later, I'd see the offending legislator and still be upset about the comments made on the floor. I might have ignored the person or even made a sarcastic comment while passing by. It made me really unhappy, and it certainly didn't win me any new friends.

These days, I can laugh about almost anything. And boy, am I a lot happier because of it. Rather than storming around my office (which is small, so it wasn't much fun storming in tiny little circles over and over), I can make a lighthearted joke about a colleague's speech or vote and move right on. It's allowed me to keep working on the issues that I care about without bringing all sorts of baggage with me, and it's opened up more opportunities for me to work with people who are different from me.

How can you go from being a tightly wound crusader for justice to a relaxed, comfortable, engaged political activist? I think you start by taking yourself a little less seriously and then realize that while the work you are doing is important, you're not exactly brokering world peace at this very moment. In other words, you're not all that.

As Americans, we tend to be rather egotistical. (This is a bit of an understatement, but you get what I'm talking about.) We, as a culture, have focused a lot of energy on ourselves. This leads us quickly to a myopic vision of the world, one in which "I am right and you are wrong." Sticking with this worldview not only saddles us with wrongheaded wars that last forever and a day, but it causes many of us to get very attached to our own ideas and beliefs, which makes us act and look like jerks. So, if we practice spending a little time each day paying attention to the people around us and thinking about things from their point of view—and maybe even considering the radical notion that their ideas might have just as much merit and value to them as our ideas do to us—we can back off a bit from that precipice of the tightly wound crusader.

I don't mean that we should all of a sudden abandon our principles and adopt moral relativism. I just mean that we should *consider* the idea that *perhaps* people with views different from our own came about those ideas honestly and that those ideas aren't *inherently* evil. Once we begin to practice this exercise regularly, we can move to the next step: that of loosening our death grip on our own ideas and realizing that our ideas are just that—ideas. They're not us, and they're not always perfect. Realizing the separateness between our ideas and ourselves, and other people's ideas and their own selves, makes it much easier to shrug off statements we don't like and laugh or smile our way to the next meeting.

Don't Take It Personally

A good way to keep friends in politics is to remember that nothing's personal. It's just politics. You're never going to agree with anyone on every single issue, so accept that right from the start. Sometimes your colleagues will do things that you think are just plain wrong, but remembering that they're not doing them *to you* will keep you sane. Sometimes they'll even make statements—possibly about you—that make your blood boil. But most times, politics is like theater. It's full of sound and fury, signifying nothing—except a headline. Keeping your head cool and not getting worked up about someone else's actions or comments will keep you on the path of making and keeping friends.

Staying calm can be especially difficult when you're working in a coalition. Some coalitions set ground rules with members about behavior, statements, and the order in which people speak during meetings. Most coalitions, though, are more of a free-for-all. People show up and participate when they can, but their first loyalty is to their own endeavors, separate and apart from the coalition's work. In these coalitions, one coalition member is bound to offend another, usually within a week. Sometimes, within minutes. (These are the *fun* coalitions!) But taking someone else's comments or actions personally is a recipe for losing. Whether you're working to make friends with one person with whom you might be in a coalition in the future or you're struggling to make friends with lots of new people in an existing coalition, personal affronts are always a major roadblock.

Here's the key point to remember: it's not about you. I know that many of us *want* it to be about us. Truth is, I pretty much always want it to be about me. But it's not. And when I try to make it about me, I lose sight of what I'm really trying to accomplish. Making friends with people who are different from you requires that you recognize that these people, sad as it may be, do not wake up in the morning thinking about you. They don't give speeches with you in mind. They don't make deals while considering how it will make you feel. In fact, they probably think about you a whole lot less than you stew about what they said or did.

Stepping back when a colleague or coalition partner does or says something you find hurtful and looking at it from a spectator's view is often helpful. Because the outside world knows that these things aren't to be taken personally, you should become a part of this outside world in your own head and look in at your situation. Removing yourself from the middle of the statement or the action can help you clearly see the situation for what it is. And what it is isn't you. Once you see the situation through the eyes of a bystander, you can watch it unfold without feeling like it's *you* doing the unfolding. Then you can decide, from the place of a watchful bystander, what if anything you want to do about the situation. This takes practice, of course, because you first have to recognize that it's happening and then choose to remove yourself and watch from the outside before reacting (or not). But it can be done and is done successfully by politicians, activists, and other people the world over.

Personally, I've learned to do it in debates with colleagues on a variety of issues. I used to get upset during debates and become righteously indignant about whatever the other person said that was so personally offensive to me. I'd launch right into a diatribe about the issue, coming across as shrill and angry. That was really dumb of me because being shrill and angry doesn't exactly win over people. Instead, it makes them run in the other direction. Once I realized this, I began practicing the art of *not taking it personally*. Now when a debate opponent takes a jab at me or says something hurtful, I try to mentally step back, remind myself it's not about me, and then get right back on track with my talking points. This lets me come across as poised, smart, and friendly. Which, not surprisingly, people like. And when people like my attitude, my style, and my demeanor, they're more likely to listen to what I say and like that too.

• • •

Making friends isn't always easy. It almost always involves your taking some sort of risk—walking across the room, listening to a viewpoint different from your own, or maybe talking about something personal in your life. The rewards for taking that risk, though, are great. For once you've mastered the skill of making friends, you can begin to form lasting coalitions with all these newfound pals.

Tips for Making Friends

Here are a few of the tips I've learned while making friends.

1. **Talk to them.** It's okay. They mostly don't bite.

2. **Listen to them.** I mean really listen, not the fake listening where you're just smiling and nodding and making your grocery list in your head.

3. **Find common ground.** You must have *something* in common with the other person. If the sole thing you have in common is the fact that you're standing in the same place talking to each other at that very moment, then start there and don't stop.

4. **Find their humanity.** It's there; you just have to look for it. And if you can't find it, then take some time to find humanity in yourself. Once you have found yours, try again with the other person. I bet you'll find it this time.

5. **Loosen up.** This one speaks for itself.

6. **Don't take it personally.** It is not all about you. To quote a great line from the film *Fight Club*, "You are not a beautiful and unique snowflake."[10] To interpret: the only person thinking about you is you. Get over it.

Letting Go
of
Outcomes

Since we're so smart and have all the answers to the world's problems, you'd think that we progressives would get more done. But sadly, we spend a lot of our time yelling in the corner that the prevailing idea or project or bill is a bad one and the one that we've painstakingly created over the course of three years, complete with charts and graphs in a shiny plastic binder, is infinitely better. And really, it should be appreciated. Meanwhile, the compromise package moves forward and wins while we stand forlornly with our three hundred shiny copies of the "good" plan. In this chapter, I posit to you, dear reader, that our obsession with specific, predetermined outcomes limits our ability to find real working solutions that appeal to a broad swath of America.

This chapter is a scary one because it advocates that we put down those shiny plastic binders, store away the charts and graphs, and let go of our predetermined outcomes. By *outcome*, I mean the thing that you just *know* will fix the problem du jour. Your seventy-two-page proposal to solve America's health-care crisis. Your treatise on the solution to the Southwest's water shortage. Your plan to ensure that every American kid leaves the third grade knowing how to read. Whatever it is, it's your outcome. It's predetermined, and you think that it is *the way*.

These proposed outcomes are usually full of pretty great ideas. Lots of them could actually work and do a lot to solve

87

real problems. So why put down your outcome? Because it's *your* outcome—not anyone else's. While you've clearly bought into it (because you dreamt it up and did all the work to create the plan), no one else has bought into it. And if you need a coalition of people to help you enact some sort of solution to a given problem, you're going to need buy-in. Sometimes, you can actually find the buy-in you need for your predetermined outcome. In these limited instances, I say, "Bully for you." Your coalition is likely made up of the *choir*—an affectionate term I use to describe the six other people who already believe exactly what you believe (also referred to as the *base*). But if that's all you need to accomplish your goal, then collect the choir and go for it.

More often, though, you're going to need much more than the choir. In fact, you're probably going to need some of those newfound friends who are very different from you. And if you need those folks, your charts and graphs and shiny plastic binders are not going to cut it. To create and maintain a working coalition with these people, you're going to have to let go of your attachment to outcomes and focus instead on your shared values and common interests. (There's more on these two topics in chapters 7 and 8.)

Why, you say? Because the conservative folks you're meeting with are just not that into your graphs and charts. They don't think that your proposal to address the crumbling infrastructure of the local transportation system is quite the thing. And they sure didn't show up to rubber-stamp your idea. They agree that the local transportation system needs an upgrade because traffic congestion is getting out of hand, but they think your solution is the pits. Your proposal calls for an increased licensing fee on SUVs and large trucks to pay for bike lanes, increased bus routes, and a new rail line connecting two suburbs. The conservatives are sitting across from you at the conference table with their mouths open, aghast at your naïveté and utter neglect of highways and freeways. Meanwhile, they've got a proposal that makes you want to move to another country, stat. They're proposing a toll road system to raise the money to build four new freeways and increase lanes on sixty-two highways throughout the metro area. The meeting quickly turns to accusations involving terms like *gas guzzler* and *tree hugger*. At the end of the day, you've got nothing but a lot of anger and a still-crumbling transportation system.

Sound familiar? It should, because it happened last week somewhere in your city.

The Art of Letting Go

Letting go of outcomes is really hard to do at first. Some people liken their great solutions to their firstborn children and treat them as such. (Think Hillary Clinton and health care, circa 1993.) While they dearly love their proposals with the tidy perfect outcomes, those proposals almost always go down in flames. Remembering this while preparing to let go of outcomes makes it easier to actually let go. Think of it this way: you can have a great idea in a fancy plastic cover that will soon be covered in dust, or you can get something done.

Jeremy Kalin understands when to let go and get things done. Jeremy is a state legislator in Minnesota. Before his successful election in 2006, Jeremy did what many young people do—he left home and went to college. Originally from Minnesota, he studied architecture in New Mexico until learning of the death of Paul Wellstone. Paul's death served as a personal wake-up call for Jeremy to "do more" than he'd been doing with his life, so he packed up and moved home to Minnesota, embarking on a new phase of life as an environmental activist.[1]

Shortly after moving back to Chisago County, he and some fellow community members attended a workshop hosted by the Conservation Fund's Gateway Community Program (a program that helps communities "protect their resources, preserve local character, and support economic growth"[2]). The workshop was designed to help the local community learn how to balance its rapid growth with preservation of the local lakes, rivers, and wildlife management area. Jeremy took some important folks with him to this workshop: a county commissioner, a former state parks planner, a member of the county planning commission, and several local business owners. They emerged from the workshop with an action plan to manage growth and economic development in Chisago County while protecting and preserving the federally designated wild and scenic rivers and surrounding open space.

Little did they know that another group, concerned with the same issue, had formed: Taxpayers for Responsible Land Use. Its name sounded ominous to a group of environmentalists.

This other group had recently rallied against the county's actions to place an emergency moratorium on the subdivision of land in the county, and their hackles rose at the mention of the word *environmentalists*. Not daunted, Jeremy and his team saw an opportunity to form a coalition when they learned about this group, and they took it. The two groups began meeting weekly at a local coffee shop. The early meetings were marked by suspicion, mistrust, and outright hostility. But over time, the group meetings relaxed into a place where people could exchange ideas and hash out plans.

In the end, the groups merged and became the Chisago County Land Use Coalition. They eventually saw almost every single proposal that they brought to the planning commission and county board adopted unanimously—their end goal of preserving open space and increasing economic value to the county achieved. How did they get from hostility to shared victory? They let go of their outcomes. Here's exactly how they got it done.

The groups traded ideas for quite some time without any real movement toward agreement. They spent much of their meetings showing each other data to support their positions without making any real progress toward a shared solution. Everyone was interested in getting to an end goal, but all were stuck in their own ideas of how to get there.

One Monday morning, the leader of Taxpayers for Responsible Land Use arrived at the coffee shop with a sketch of a plan to divide some open space land into three-acre lots, each lot designed for personal home construction. He tossed the plan on the table and said to Jeremy, "It's only three-acre lots, not four, but take a look if you want to." You see, the leader of the group didn't think that Jeremy or the other environmental activists would seriously consider any division of land that broke up personal lots into smaller spaces—he'd assumed that Jeremy wanted large, spacious lots for each purchaser in the area. Jeremy grabbed the sketch, took a cursory look, and said, "No, of course we can't agree to that." Typically, environmentalists oppose plans and proposals to divide large swaths of open space into smaller, developed tracts of land. Taxpayers for Responsible Land Use wanted to parcel the open space into residential tracts; Jeremy wanted to preserve some pristine open space. The two seemed headed back to square one.

But a few moments later, Jeremy grabbed the sketch and thought while looking at it. He then suggested to the Taxpayer that they consider "clustering"—putting eight houses on one acre of land so that the unused land could be saved for conservation. This was a brand new idea, one that neither the so-called enviros nor the Taxpayer had thought of before. The Taxpayer was surprised by the idea but intrigued.

The Taxpayer went off to research clustering and came back several weeks later willing to move forward with the idea. He expressed surprise once again that the enviros would go for an idea where homes had only one-eighth-acre lots and said so to Jeremy. But finally, Jeremy and the Taxpayer had connected about what they each really wanted: Jeremy wanted to conserve as much land as possible while being economically viable, and the Taxpayer wanted home values to stay high and business to thrive in the region. By letting go of their predetermined ideas about what the conservation plan "had" to look like—and by letting go of their preconceptions about what the other group would think about these ideas—they were able to creatively come up with an idea that met everyone's interests.

Everyone Loses When We Refuse to Let Go

As we're all painfully aware, not all coalition stories end this nicely with such tidy outcomes. When we refuse to let go of outcomes and push stubbornly for our one predetermined answer to a given problem, we often see poor results. Failure is the most common result, and on those occasions when your proposed solution "wins," you've left some scorched earth behind you.

David Fulmer encountered a loss a few years ago when he refused to let go of outcomes. David is a fire chief in Ohio today, but a few years ago he was the fire chief in a suburb of Madison, Wisconsin. He'd been hired by the mayor of the city, who was defeated in a reelection bid less than a year after David's arrival. The change in city leadership left David in the hands of the new mayor, a former city council member. The new mayor's first order of business was to instruct David to merge the city's fire service with the local EMS (emergency medical service). You see, the city was part of a joint EMS district with two adjacent communities. The three communities shared the cost of the service and were supposed to share the benefits of the service. But prior to David's arrival, his city had been growing, and growing much faster than the other two communities. So while David's city paid 60 percent of the EMS contract, it wasn't getting 60 percent of the services anymore.

The mayor's idea made a lot of sense to David. The EMS contract was costly, and it would be much cheaper to pull out of the EMS agreement and fold the EMS personnel into his fire department. Then the fire department could provide round-the-clock fire and emergency medical services (the fire department was staffed only on weekdays at the time) to the city at a lower cost overall. David, being the newly minted master of public administration that he was, set about crunching the numbers and developing the transition plan. And boy, did he create a great plan. It was less expensive, provided better, faster, and more comprehensive service to the city; and just made sense.

David took his plan to the mayor. The mayor loved it, as did the city manager. Next David went in front of the city council to present his plan. The council members torpedoed him within minutes. David's carefully crafted plan went up in smoke, right there during the public meeting.

And why? Well, David didn't have any relationships with the political decision makers in the city. He never talked to any of the city council members before the night of his presentation to gauge their reactions to his proposal. Turns out, one of the city council members had sat on the EMS advisory council for years and felt a commitment to the entire district. He wasn't willing to back out of the agreement and leave the two other, smaller communities holding a 60 percent increase in the cost of services. Another member of the

EMS advisory council was a prominent member of the city David worked for. This member also didn't want to support a plan that would leave the other two communities high and dry. The city had been a part of this EMS district for well over twenty years, and it wasn't about to skip town on the team. Unfortunately, David didn't know any of this until after his proposal was trashed.

David's big mistake was that he clung too tightly to his outcome—merging the fire department with the EMS. What the mayor really wanted from David was to increase the city's capacity to meet the residents' emergency needs and decrease costs. Yet both David and the mayor had determined that the way to achieve these goals was to merge the two services. But was that the only way?

In retrospect, David told me that he didn't explore other options and that perhaps he would have explored those ideas if he'd worked more with the city council, the EMS advisory council, and other interested parties. David left that city after only a few years and moved on to other places. But the lesson learned there was clear for him: because he was set on one outcome and didn't work creatively with others to find a solution that worked for everyone, the city got no solution at all.

We've all made this mistake many times; if not in coalition work, we've all certainly done it in our personal lives. But the lessons from both are the same: when you come to the table ready to let go of your specific, predetermined outcomes and are open to the possibility of something new, coalitions can flourish and win.

BONUS BOX

How to Let Go of Outcomes

Letting go can be hard! Here are two easy steps to help you let go.

1. **Release your grip on the shiny plastic binder**—or whatever the plastic shiny binder looks like in your life. Translation: if you've already made up your mind about what the outcome "should" be, take a moment to trash that outcome because it isn't going to happen.

2. **Open your mind to the new.** Hold in your head for a moment the idea that the solution to the problem you're addressing may actually be in someone else's head. Now go ask other people about their ideas.

Getting Back to Our Shared Values

As progressives, we often focus so much on specific issues that we forget to plan or act from a values-based perspective. While we're spending all of our energy trying to convince people how important it is to support public education or environmental protection, we're forgetting just *why* we care so much about education and the environment. It's easy for rational, good-hearted people to disagree on an issue. It's less easy for us to disagree on our values because we largely share the same ones. And now that we've let go of our obsession with outcomes, we can learn to connect again with progressive values—values that are nearly universal and motivate all of us to do what we do.

Why Values Are Important to Coalition Work

First, what are values? We learned in chapter 6 that outcomes are the things that we have decided are the solutions to given problems. They involve predetermined paths and bills and action plans that we've usually dreamt up by ourselves in a small, quiet room somewhere. An outcome belongs to you, and usually to you alone. Values, on the other hand, are core beliefs and principles in which people have an emotional investment. Some examples of values are freedom, opportunity, security, fairness, equality, safety, and protection. Values are fairly universal—we humans all share a core set of values, even though we define and demonstrate them in different ways.

Why focus on values? Since we all generally have the same core values, we can use those values as a base for building a sustainable, functional, and winning coalition. Rather than fighting over whether Person A's outcome is a better solution than Person B's outcome, when we focus on values we eschew outcomes in favor of common ground as a starting place for our work. Using shared values as a base for working together is really helpful when a coalition involves people who aren't all exactly alike. And if you want a coalition that is bigger than six people, you're probably going to need some value talk to get you started.

Progressives have a hard time talking about values. We tend to be rather wonkish, so we jump straight to our policy ideas (read: *outcomes*). We get irritated at the Right for talking in such broad generalities and desperately want to show our facts and figures to the public, for that surely will prove us right and them wrong! But the reason that members of the Right have done well in the past forty years is, they've been talking about values. I certainly don't agree with the *way* they've been talking about values, but I can't deny that they've been doing one heck of a job at it. While we talk about the number of children living without health care in the United States today and the intricate details of a single-payer health-care system, they've been talking about personal responsibility, a core American value. Some have used the core value of personal responsibility as a reason to oppose movement toward expansion of health care, which you and I probably disagree with, but it's been done pretty well over the last twenty years. Meanwhile, activists on the left have failed to connect their numbers and detailed health-care consolidation plans to another core American value: shared responsibility, or stewardship.

It's not easy to focus on values, and even when we manage to do so in order to work more effectively with new partners and potential allies, those around us may get nervous, upset, or even hostile. Early attempts by the New Mexico Wilderness Alliance to use values as a base for forming unlikely coalitions met with some interesting opposition.

In the late 1990s, Garrick Delzell worked for the New Mexico Wilderness Alliance, a nonprofit organization dedicated to the protection, restoration, and continued enjoyment of New Mexico's wildlands and wilderness areas. The group seeks to protect remaining wilderness in the state through administrative designation, advocacy, and federal wilderness designation. Today, the group comprises local conservation groups and organizations, local businesses, and over six thousand individual members throughout the state and has established a reputation for working in broad-based coalitions to achieve its goals.[1]

But back in the late 1990s, the organization was new and just starting to work on wilderness preservation. It began with a major project aimed at setting aside two hundred thousand acres of wilderness for preservation and hired Garrick Delzell as its first wilderness protection organizer. Garrick took a look at his state and decided to meet with the ranchers. New Mexico is home to thousands of ranchers—they make up the single largest constituency of landowners in the rural areas of the state and wield heavy influence over the state's

decisions regarding land and water. To Garrick, it made perfect sense to talk to the ranchers. Not only did he know that
the alliance would need their support for its fledgling effort
to set aside two hundred thousand acres for preservation in
the state, but he also saw ranchers as natural allies of the
conservation community. In short, he believed that ranchers
and conservationists shared some basic values, such as
respect for the land, a desire to keep the land healthy and
productive for future generations, and stewardship over the
land and wildlife.

Garrick began traveling the state and talking with ranchers,
forming relationships with them and learning about their
concerns and interests. After several months, he'd established trust with a number of ranchers and felt like things
were really coming together. However, during board reports,
a minority of board members expressed concern about his
close relationships with the ranchers, relying on historical
divisions (real or perceived) between the conservation and
the ranching communities. Garrick was encouraged to spend
less time working with the ranchers and more time on traditional environmental protection activities. The relationship
between the alliance and the ranchers withered. When it
came time to actually set aside the land targeted for preservation, only about ten thousand of the two hundred thousand acres of targeted land were protected. Garrick moved
on to another job, and the alliance kept working to preserve
the state's land a bit at a time. Over time, the alliance changed
the way it functioned, and now one visiting New Mexico
would see New Mexico Wilderness Alliance staff and board

members working closely with ranchers throughout the state, with greater results and better prospects for long-term preservation of land.

Garrick understood that while ranchers and conservationists had historically spoken different languages in New Mexico, advocating divergent outcomes to solve the state's land and wildlife problems and using distinct terminology to talk about both the problems and the proposed solutions, they—at the core of their belief systems—share the same values. Both groups care deeply about the land, the animals that live on the land, and the vegetation that grows on the land. They care about the future of the land. And so Garrick's attempt to bring these two groups to a common space rested fundamentally on a values-based strategy. Garrick made inroads with the ranchers because he put aside outcomes and talked about the values they shared. And if that work had continued, the conservation community may well have joined forces with the ranching community years sooner than it actually did in New Mexico.

How to Talk About Values Instead of Outcomes

It's easy to say, "Okay, great, I will start using values-based language instead of outcome-based language." But go ahead and try it—right now. Say out loud to your beagle who's resting on the foot of the bed (he'll appreciate you no matter what you say), what your fundamental values are regarding education. Ten bucks says you can't do it. Actually, what I mean is: ten bucks says that when you started talking about education, you said something along the lines of "We need a good, strong public education system that teaches kids to read and gets them prepared for college." I would happen to agree with your statement, as does your beagle, but that statement is not a value. It's a position (read: *outcome*). You see, the statement sets forth the *outcome* that you want: funding and political support for a certain kind of education system (public) that accomplishes certain goals (teaches kids to read and gets them prepared for college). Not everyone agrees with your statement, as we can see daily on C-SPAN. But everyone *can* agree on a core value underneath our support for education: opportunity. We all believe that children should be afforded the *opportunity* to learn. And almost all of us believe that a child has a fundamental *right* to learn.

Barack Obama is a master at speaking the language of values rather than outcomes, which is why he was so successful not only as a state legislator and United States Senator but as a presidential candidate. He can speak to people with widely divergent views and, by using values-laden language rather than outcome-laden language, have these divergent groups all nodding their heads and stepping to the table to work together. He said it best in August 2008 during his acceptance speech as the Democratic presidential nominee at the Democratic National Convention:

> We may not agree on abortion, but surely we
> can agree on reducing the number of unwanted
> pregnancies in this country. The reality of gun

ownership may be different for hunters in rural
Ohio than for those plagued by gang-violence in
Cleveland, but don't tell me we can't uphold the
Second Amendment while keeping AK-47s out of
the hands of criminals. I know there are differences
on same-sex marriage, but surely we can agree that
our gay and lesbian brothers and sisters deserve to
visit the person they love in the hospital and to live
lives free of discrimination. Passions fly on immigration, but I don't know anyone who benefits when
a mother is separated from her infant child or an
employer undercuts American wages by hiring
illegal workers.[2]

In these four sentences, Senator Obama noted that people in
America have differing opinions on positions or outcomes
but that all people are connected together by the shared values that lie beneath those outcomes. Abortion, a hotly con-
tested issue, is put aside in favor of the values of protection
and prevention. Gun regulation is put aside for the value of
safety. The issue of gay marriage is put aside for the values
of empathy and fairness. Immigration policy is put aside for
the values of compassion and equity. As Americans, we all
share these core values. And when we choose to start our
conversations with these shared values, we are much more
likely to continue working together until we create shared
solutions.

Here are some more examples of how we can switch our
policy-heavy language into values-driven language:

Instead of:	Think of:
Increased government regulation of corporations	Transparency and honesty
No more wiretapping and government spying	Liberty and freedom
Stopping corporate greed	Fairness
Civil unions for gay couples	Security
Increased funding for education	Opportunity public
Reversing the effects of warming	Sustainability and global stewardship
Working with the UN and NATO	Cooperation and security
Increased funding for child protective services	Protection and compassion

This list could go on for days, but you get the point. Everyone will certainly not agree on the outcomes listed on the left, but we can all agree on the values listed on the right. When issues come up, people get polarized because they're attached to their idea of what the outcome should be. When we can move the discussion away from outcomes and toward values, we find common ground and can build our relationships from there.

This approach sounds so wonderful, and it is. However, it's not miraculous. It doesn't always work, at least not right away. Sometimes we can't come to an agreement even when we use values language.[3] One example in Arizona involves restoration of voting rights. Most Arizonans share some values around this issue: we believe that people have a responsibility to participate in civic life, and we believe in redemption. Whether people favor or disfavor the restoration of voting rights for convicted felons, they value responsibility and redemption. In Arizona, we haven't yet figured out how to translate those values into legislation that we can all agree on, but that doesn't mean that we won't in the future. While I favor legislation that grants automatic restoration of voting rights to all felons who've completed their duty to the state, my Republican colleague believes that we should permanently ban violent felons from voting forever. Does that mean we have different values? No. We both believe in responsibility and redemption. Right now, though, we're defining those values from different places. We need to keep working to find more common ground—and we've agreed that we will.

BONUS BOX

Talking About Values

Talking about values takes practice. Here are a few steps to get you started:

1. **Make a List.** Write down ten things that you care about (political things, not your cat or great-aunt).

2. **Organize it.** Read over your list and classify the items as issues or values. Refer to the examples in this chapter if you can't tell which is which.

3. **Don't cheat.** I know most of the items on your list are issues, so just be honest and call them issues. Don't bother trying to pretend they're values.

4. **Find the value words.** Think about what it is about the issues that makes you care about them. What is underneath? Find one or two *value* words to describe what's underneath.

5. **Look for help.** If this exercise feels impossible and frustrating, feel free to look at my list of commonly held values (see the box) and see which of them might describe your issues.

6. **Repeat.** Practice this over and over until you're able to list values instead of issues in step 1.

7. **Research.** If you keep failing at this task, put this book down and consider reading these books: George Lakoff's *Don't Think of an Elephant* and Bernie Horn's *Framing the Future*.

BONUS BOX 2

Common American Values

Here's a list of values words to get you started:

Empathy	Sustainability
Responsibility	Protection
Fairness	Freedom
Equality	Liberty
Opportunity	Democracy
Trust	Individual rights
Cooperation	Service
Compassion	Justice
Community	Fulfillment
Diversity	Honesty
Appreciation	Openness
Respect	Security
Common good	Stewardship
Accountability	Transparency

Naming Our Interests

Because we've been so obsessed with outcomes, we often forget to think about *why* we want a certain outcome or what our motivation is for naming that outcome. By skipping right to the end game, we've cut off our own creativity and ability to look at the broader picture for new possibilities. We've driven ourselves onto little dirt roads on the fringe of America, alone and separate from the rest of the country. What we really want is a great democratic paradise where all Americans can be happy, so we have to broaden our ethos to include all of America. We can include everyone if we back away from outcomes and name our values (which we just did!). Now that we've identified our values, we can figure out what our interests are in a given situation.

Arizona Together: One Coalition, Many Interests

I wrote about Arizona Together a bit in chapter 4. This was the statewide coalition formed in, you guessed it, Arizona in 2005 in order to defeat the same-sex marriage amendment initiative that was on the ballot in November 2006. When we began forming this coalition, I knew that we were going to need some unlikely allies on our side. You can't win something this big with two gay-rights groups, the ACLU (American Civil Liberties Union), and Planned Parenthood. You need the ACLU and Planned Parenthood and the gay-rights groups, absolutely, but you also need about fifty other groups too. And some of those groups have to include folks that don't eat Sunday dinner at your house.

We set about our coalition work diligently, first collecting some great tried-and-true allies who are always with us, through thick and thin. Then we started reaching out to the folks whom you wouldn't expect to care about a same-sex marriage ban. How did we do it? By naming the interests that these unlikely allies had in ensuring that this initiative failed. Here are some of the groups we successfully recruited to the coalition and how we identified their interests:

• *K–12 schoolteachers.* Actually, K–12 schoolteachers really don't talk about marriage. It's not part of the curriculum, and it wouldn't seem likely that they'd care much one way or the other whether this initiative passed or failed— except that a number of school districts in Arizona extend health-care benefits to the partners and kids of unmarried teachers. This initiative would have eliminated the school districts' legal right to offer those benefits. So teachers had an identified interest in this coalition—protection of those health care benefits.

• *Domestic violence shelters.* Again, the topic of same-sex marriage doesn't often surface around the DV shelter table, and it's certainly not a political issue that the DV community wants to wade into. But in 2004, Ohio passed a same-sex marriage ban and the courts thereafter struck down the state's domestic violence statutes that pro-tected women from abuse by their live-in boyfriends. So domestic violence prevention advocates had an identified interest in this coalition: the protection of domestic violence laws for unmarried victims of domestic violence.

• *Police officers and firefighters.* Now, here are a couple of groups that you'd expect to run the other direction when the terms *same-sex* and *marriage* are put together. And in fact, at first it wasn't easy to approach these groups because of some of the stigma attached to the *idea* of a same-sex marriage amendment. But it turns out that a lot of police officers and firefighters (firefighters in particular) shack up. I can't tell you why, but a good number of male police officers and firefighters in Arizona enjoy long-term, loving relationships with their girlfriends and just never get married. Someone somewhere has probably written a thesis or doctoral dissertation on this phenomenon, but I'll leave it to you to find it and read it. All I can say is that a lot of unmarried guys spend their days protecting my life and yours. So, despite the initial hesitancy on some folks' part, I was able to meet with the local police and firefighter groups and lay out the impact of this initiative. And their interest was revealed: these guys (and a few gals) had health-care plans (thanks to their unions, of course) that provided the same benefits and protections to their partners and children that the married police officers and firefighters enjoyed. And the initiative, if passed, would take those benefits away. The unions in particular saw this as an immediate decrease in their bargaining power—one less benefit to provide for their members.

- *Retired folks.* We have a whole lot of retired people in Arizona. (It really is the weather.) Luckily for them, a lot of these retirees find love again in later life and get to spend their last days with someone they love. Often, they choose not to get married. Sometimes it's because they'll lose their Social Security benefits if they remarry, other times a widow doesn't want to risk losing her deceased husband's pension, and sometimes a widower chooses not to remarry out of respect for his beloved but gone wife. Whatever the reason may be, Sun City is full of unmarried love. And when we met with the Arizona Association of Retired Americans, its members understood their interest in this initiative quite quickly, and they signed on to the coalition.

- *Businesses.* Most major corporations in America offer domestic partner health benefits. In response to a growing number of unmarried families in the United States, corporations have realized that they need to offer competitive health benefits for employees' family members in order to attract and retain the best talent possible. And although the Arizona marriage initiative stated on its face that it would eliminate only the government's ability to recognize these unmarried families, businesses had heard the rumors—that it would take only one little lawsuit after the passage of an amendment like this and businesses that contract with the state or interact with the state financially would also be required to cut off benefits to their unmarried employees. Businesses felt a keen interest in joining the coalition—the interest of their pocketbook.

The list could go on for pages, but it's clear from these examples that the key to Arizona Together's great coalition breadth was its ability and willingness to identify the interest of every group involved—and then find a way to meet that interest. If the campaign had chosen to stick with identity politics or had focused on only what the gay community thought the outcome should look like, this coalition would never have been possible. But because we let go of preconceived notions of what the campaign coalition "had to" or "should" look like, we were able to bring a much larger group of people to the table and win a decisive and historic victory.

How to Name Your Interests

Once you've identified a group of people with whom you share values, you can set about the work of naming your respective interests and moving toward shared outcomes that everyone can buy into. Rather than coming with your own preconceived notions of how this whole matter will turn out, you name your interests—those things that you care about deeply and that are based on your values. However, sometimes people have a hard time distinguishing between outcomes (bad) and interests (good).

Here's the difference. An outcome is a "product" that you're attached to and that usually is articulated as a specific "thing" you want to have happen. Here's an example of an outcome: *The school district should pay more for staff health-care plans.* Outcomes are polarizing because others at the coalition table may not, and probably will not, agree with your specific outcome. Fights happen and the coalition breaks up. An interest, on the other hand, is a general commitment to a principle that guides your work and reason for being involved in the coalition. There are lots of ways to meet an interest but only one way to meet an outcome. Here's an example of an interest: *Staff should have access to high-quality health care*. See how the two statements are different? The first *demands* that the school district allocate more of its limited budget to pay for the health-care plans of its staff. The second statement leaves open lots of avenues to address the issue of health care for staff. The first limits discussion and collaboration because it articulates an *end*. The second spurs debate and creative, collaborative ideas because it articulates a *beginning*.

Switching from operating in an outcome-based framework to operating in an interest-based framework takes practice and dedication. Coalitions that flourish are almost always groups that have made the transition successfully. Here's an example: Grow Montana is a broad-based coalition in, of course, Montana. Grow Montana has articulated its purpose, which is "to promote community economic development policies that support sustainable Montana-owned food production, processing, and distribution, and that improve all of our citizens' access to Montana foods."[1] The project claims members from the Left, such as Alternative Energy Resources and the Montana Organic Association; from the Right, like the Montana Grain Growers Association and the Montana Farm Bureau; and from groups in between, like the Montana

Farmers Union and Montana Foodbank Network. The coalition focuses on legislative and administrative policy changes in the state to encourage local food production and consumption. Historically, these disparate groups hadn't worked together in the state.

In 2005, a small group of folks interested in creating such a coalition began a fledgling effort to bring together people interested in food production, sale, and sustainability and started talking about their common values. Turns out that everyone at the table wanted to increase local food production and distribution. Some groups were interested in this because they represented local growers or ranchers. Others were invested in the global sustainability movement and believed that local production and distribution was good for the planet. Still other groups supported local efforts from a health perspective (if you know where your food comes from, you can trust what's in it). I talked to Crissie McMullan, who works for Grow Montana, and asked her how the coalition managed to bring so many historically divergent groups together to accomplish some pretty ambitious goals.

She said that Grow Montana managed to bring everyone together when the coalition leaders articulated a common goal that met every group's interests. Together, the member organizations agreed that approaching policy changes around food production and distribution would be best received from an economic development perspective. It took some time for Grow Montana to find agreement on this strategy, but Crissie said that when articulating everyone's *interests* in local food production and distribution, the coalition found that everyone shared an interest in local economic development. Once it found this nexus, the coalition set out to pass legislation that would advance its goals. Here are some examples of its highly successful 2007 legislative session:

- *Montana Food to Institutions.* This bill provided an optional exemption from the state procurement act to allow public institutions to buy Montana-grown food. (The pre-2007 law required the institutions to buy the cheapest food available, regardless of where it was grown.)[2]

- *Value-Added Food Production Study.* This legislation established a state study committee to research ways that Montana can increase its value-added food production (of meat, for example) so that Montanans can buy and eat local foods. This would keep profits in Montana and contribute to the state's economic development.[3]

- *Resolution to Remove Ban on Interstate Commerce of State-Inspected Meat.* This resolution asked Congress to remove the U.S. Department of Agriculture's ban on interstate commerce of meat inspected in Montana. Federal requirements limited the ability of local farmers to sell their state-inspected meat to a wider market, thus limiting economic development in the state.[4]

Each of the three bills passed almost unanimously and was signed by Governor Brian Schweitzer (a farmer himself!). The coalition has continued to grow over the last year and maintains its broad membership through the strategic use of coalition partners' interests in the decision-making process.

Each policy directive that Grow Montana eventually chooses relates to member groups' various interests. How does Grow Montana know this? The members spend time articulating their interests in the ultimate agenda (which is, of course, to promote local food production and consumption) and then choose legislation that meets the interests of all the parties. For example, the Montana Food to Institutions bill met the interests of the farmers, who want to sell their products; the organic food producers, who also want to sell their products (which they had a hard time doing before because organics are sometimes more expensive); the local growers' associations, who want to increase in-state sales; and the sustainability partners, who are interested in reducing transportation costs, pollution, energy expenditure, and other costs associated with transporting food across state lines for sale. The coalition was able to support the bill unanimously because the bill met the interests of all parties. And importantly, the group started the process by collecting everyone's interests and *then* choosing a policy agenda that brought those interests together.

Grow Montana is a great example of how to effectively use interests to set a shared agenda within a coalition and achieve it. By repeatedly returning to their interests (rather than getting attached to outcomes), the group members were able to choose three goals and achieve each of them.

BONUS BOX

How to Utilize Interests in Coalition Work

It's tricky work identifying, remembering, and utilizing your interests. Use these questions to keep you on track.

1. **What are my values?** Remind yourself of the values underlying your work in a given coalition. Refer to chapter 7 if you find yourself naming issues or outcomes instead of values.

2. **What's my interest?** Using your values as a guide, determine what *interest* you have in the project your coalition is working on. Name that interest out loud to the group.

3. **Are we meeting my interest?** When moving toward options for action, keep your interest on the table. Evaluate all options for progress to see if they meet your interest.

4. **Have I gotten stuck on outcomes?** If you find yourself getting stuck in the coalition's work without a resolution, check to make sure you're still operating from an interest, not an outcome. Remember that there are lots of ways to meet an interest, but only one way to meet an outcome.

The Third Way

Once we've loosened our vicelike grip on outcomes and identity politics, identified our shared values, and named our interests, we can work together to create good policy that works for all of us. Because we've let go of our preconceived notions of what the "right" versus the "wrong" answers are to our questions, we can find shared outcomes together. I call this process of letting go and discovering outcomes together the Third Way.[1] It's a way of working in coalition with others that defies much of today's political mode of operation. Rather than scheming and sneaking to gain the upper hand, the members of a Third Way coalition trust each other, share similar values, name their interests at the outset, identify their shared goal, and then work toward it as a team. Although this is somewhat rare to see, it can and does happen. Here's an example.

The Third Way in Action

Mark Wendelsdorf and his coalition used the Third Way after 9/11 when lots of other communities relied on old, tired political maneuvering and petty infighting. Mark is the fire chief in Caldwell, Idaho, which sits in a rural area of the state. (Actually, most of Idaho is rural.) Back in the 1990s, Caldwell was designated as the "house" for the haz-mat team for that region. (For those of us who haven't carved out a career in daily lifesaving activities, *haz-mat* is industry lingo for hazardous materials or hazardous materials response team.)

Prior to 9/11, the Caldwell Fire Department had basic funding to put a haz-mat team together. The haz-mat team responded whenever the local law enforcement and fire teams couldn't handle a given hazardous situation. But after 9/11, the situation changed. Federal dollars were allocated around the country from the Centers for Disease Control (CDC), the Department of Health Services, and the Federal Emergency Management Agency as a result of congressional action to prepare the country against future attacks.

Shortly after the money started to flow, news outlets around the country were reporting incidents of localities making duplicate purchases, buying equipment and putting it in storage without knowing how to use it, and more. In more populated areas of the country, law enforcement, hospitals, health districts, and fire districts were not coordinating with each other; instead, each spent its federally apportioned money however it wanted to. The story spreading across the country was that these dollars weren't going to do any good, that they were being wasted.

But the problems weren't happening just in urban areas. Right next door to Mark, in Oregon, the local haz-mat team asked the state to order some special equipment for it, but the state had already decided that it would choose what to order for all the local teams. This meant that the emergency response teams in East Oregon weren't getting the materials they needed, and they weren't prepared for all the emergency situations they might encounter.

However, in Idaho, each local community had been granted the power to make decisions that best fit it. And in Mark's community, he formed a coalition with the local health district chair. Because Idaho isn't a highly populated area, they knew that they wouldn't get a huge portion of the federal money coming from Congress like the major urban centers would get. They also knew that they needed to work together to make their dollars stretch farther and have the impact they were intended to have: to protect their region of the country from future unknown emergencies. So Mark and the health district chair called together all the regional hospitals, fire departments, police departments, health districts, emergency managers (EMS teams), the Idaho State Department of Agriculture, the Idaho State Police, the Idaho Bureau of Homeland Security, all the state labs, and Idaho's Civil Support Team.

All member groups came to the table without predetermined wants or ideas of how they wanted to spend their portion of the federal funds (hint: these would be outcomes) and instead agreed on a shared value: ensuring safety and security for their community. With safety and security in mind, they discussed their interests, which were all pretty similar. Each member group wanted to ensure that the money apportioned to the community was spent in as practical a manner as possible to help as many people as possible and with as little waste as possible. (These people in Idaho are so genuine. In other places, like perhaps Chicago, I think we might see some folks with different interests, such as getting rich—or powerful.)

The member groups pooled all the money that had been allocated to them from the various federal entities and then decided purchasing priorities as a group, regardless of where that money would actually be spent or who would have "ownership" of the equipment purchased. This is a pretty big commitment to make, especially by small rural departments already struggling to make ends meet. But they were very committed to their shared goal: providing the best service to the community in the event of an emergency or disaster.

For example, the coalition spent some of the health district's money from the CDC on equipment to help the fire departments respond immediately at the scene of an incident because the money that had been formally allocated to the departments couldn't be spent on the equipment that the fire departments actually needed. And when the group realized that they weren't prepared to respond to a mass contamination incident, they asked the state to pay for the regional haz-mat materials and spent their federal dollars on decon equipment (that's *decontamination*, for us regular folks) and mass-casualty equipment for the local hospitals to use in the field.

As the coalition members worked together, they became closer over time, not only because they made major decisions together, but also because this process created trust among group members. By May 2005, the group was working very well together, engaging in coordinated drills and making further purchasing decisions based on their experiences in these drills. They had become a well-functioning coalition, where member groups trusted each other, worked well together, and could count on each other to fulfill the group's goals.

On July 7, 2005, their coalition work paid off. Sometime in the early afternoon, a 911 call came in concerning some sick farmworkers in a field in rural Idaho. Paramedics were sent out to the scene and determined that the workers had all been exposed to a pesticide in the field and were in critical condition. The firefighters on the scene did a quick decon of the workers they encountered, but shortly learned that thirty-four other farmworkers were in or near the area, all of whom were also getting very sick.

The coalition dispatched the haz-mat team and the decon unit to the field. Within ten minutes, the decon unit was processing people through the outdoor decon unit they'd purchased with their federal allocation and the haz-mat team was preparing to transport people to local hospitals for further treatment. The entire coalition jumped on a phone call together so all the area hospitals would know that thirty-six people had been exposed to pesticides out in this field. The hospitals began to prepare to receive the patients, while the local police and the State Department of Agriculture began researching the source of the pesticide. To complicate matters, the contaminated farmworkers were all monolingual Spanish speakers, so the coalition needed to find translators. One of the member groups called some local farmworker advocacy organizations to come translate instructions to the farmworkers and ensure that they were informed about what was happening.

Within twenty minutes, the police and Department of Agriculture had identified the field in which the workers were exposed, and determined which pesticide had been sprayed the night before. By this time, the farmworkers had all been decontaminated and were receiving emergency medical care at the scene of the exposure. Meanwhile, Mark, the fire chief, had called the hospital coalition representative and asked for its hospital's media liaison to handle all media calls and interactions. Television stations arrived at the field within thirty minutes of the 911 call, but since they didn't find any sick, naked workers lying in the fields, media coverage focused on the successful treatment of the contaminated workers. What could have been a media disaster was instead a story highlighting how quickly and safely the problem had been resolved. All the farmworkers were transported to local hospitals, treated, taken home, and monitored for days afterward. Not a single worker suffered any long-term damage from the exposure because the coalition had done exactly what it had been formed to do: provide safety and security to the community in the case of emergencies.

Mark's coalition functioned in the Third Way. Coalition members came together for a larger purpose, a shared goal. They willingly put aside their own ideas about specific outcomes and instead focused on their shared values. They made decisions based on group members' interests, and they did so without regard to ownership or even respective positions of power. During the whole coalition formation process, they spent time forming meaningful relationships based on trust. Then, when the time came to deliver on their ultimate goal, they did so without fault. This is the Third Way.[2]

Tips to Stay in the Third Way

Here's a cheat sheet of the steps you can take to stay in the Third Way.

1. **Dump identity politics.** It stands in the way of your work and keeps your coalition small and narrow.

2. **Make friends.** Learn to trust and work with people who are different from you and whom you need to be successful.

3. **Let go of outcomes.** Throw out the predetermined ideas of what you think the coalition should do and what you think the coalition should "get" at the end of your work.

4. **Name your values.** Talk about what your underlying values are instead of naming the issue and citing all of the fancy facts supporting your issue.

5. **Name your interest.** Figure out why you're at the coalition table, and evaluate the coalition's proposed work to see if the shared plan meets your interests.

6. **Trust.** Believe that your other coalition partners are doing the same. If they're not, talk about it—nicely.

7. **Get to work!**

10

And,
Not But

I remember when I was a kid and my parents told me to do this or that. Invariably, I'd respond with "But, Dad—," and invariably, the response was "No buts." I was constantly frustrated with this response and yet had no recourse. I knew that I had something earth-shatteringly important to say to my parents that would absolutely change their minds about the issue under discussion, and I had no way to communicate it. I was stuck.

Only years later did I learn that the magic word ending those discussions was *but*. *But* is an interesting word. The definition of *but* is "on the contrary." Every time we speak that word, we are saying "No, that isn't right." Not a great way to start a dialogue, is it? If you're looking for common ground, if you're seeking a Third Way, *but* is about the worst word in the English language to use. It creates an immediate barrier between the people attempting to communicate with each other. When I said the word *but* to my parents, they knew what was coming: a teenager's extremely well-thought-out argument why a curfew of 10:00 p.m. was completely unreasonable, with a host of twenty reasons and examples showing why, followed by a brief episode of pouting and hating the entire world. No wonder they shut down any discussion and sent me to my room. I had gone about it all wrong by starting with the word *but*. Using *but* never got me what I wanted, and it always left me disappointed.

So, in grown-up land, say you're going along great in your political endeavor, working on the Most Important Initiative of the Century, and coalition partner Republicans for a Responsible Environment makes a suggestion that just infuriates the Greens for a Green Planet. The Greens for a Green Planet blurt out "But we can't do that!" in the middle of the Republicans for a Responsible Environment's proposal, and the fight is on. The Green Planet people start accusing the Responsible Environment people of being in bed with Exxon, and the Responsible Environment people respond that the Greens might as well live in a tree, for all of their practical knowledge, and the situation escalates from there. The productive work of the coalition has stalled.

When the Greens for a Green Planet yelled out the word *but*, they sent a message to the Republicans for a Responsible Environment that their proposal was wrong and bad. They shut them down before the idea had even been fully explained. Don't get me wrong. The idea might have been horrible and stupid. It might have led to the destruction of every fragile ecosystem in the country. The idea also could have been the most brilliant, innovative idea ever conjured by an environmental organization. Its implementation could have saved six million trees this year. We just don't know, though, because the Green Planet people never let the idea live, even for a moment. By immediately shutting down the Responsible Environment people with the word *but*, the Green Planet people stopped an idea that could have had some merit, damaged the relationship between the two groups, and diminished the collective power of the coalition by creating division. *But* is quite a powerful word.

At this moment, the coalition is in desperate need of the word *and*. A coalition builder watching the breakdown between the Republicans for a Responsible Environment and the Greens for a Green Planet could do what is often done (run into the next room and drink while pulling out bits of her hair), or she could save her scalp and introduce the word *and* into the discussion. Not only does the second option preserve her epidermis and internal organs, but it also brings the group back together for some creative, expansive thinking. Using the word *and* to connect the Republicans' idea to the Greens' concern can defuse the tensions in the room, rebuild the relationships between the two groups, and move the coalition forward toward a solution. Both groups' statements and concerns had validity and both groups brought important points to the table. The use of the word *and* can validate people's views while bringing them together for a greater, larger outcome that meets everyone's needs.

That's why I propose that we dump *but*. The whole word— just throw it out. In exchange, we can use the word *and*. *And* is a great word. It means "together with or along with, in addition to, as well as." It feels good just to *write* that definition. I can feel the love in the room already. No, seriously, the word *and* is a powerful tool in coalition work. *And* is used to complement, to add value to, to supplement another person's statement or idea.

What a concept. Instead of using a word that says "No, that isn't right" we instead begin using a word that says "Okay, let's put that together with this and see what we can come up with." When we use the word *and* instead of *but*, we're shifting our brains to think differently about both ourselves and those we work with. By dropping our black-and-white thinking about what is right and what is wrong, we are creating all sorts of space for new creative ideas and solutions to appear. I have seen this happen, and it produces some exciting results.

Using *And* in Darfur

During the spring of 2007, I decided that I was going to do something about Darfur. I, like many people across the country, was horrified when I learned about the genocide in Darfur several years earlier. I also felt like there was little I could do to stop it. As an American living in Phoenix, I wondered what influence I could have on a region of a country on the other side of the planet. I remembered the Rwandan genocide—which occurred in the blip of a news cycle while I was in college—and I remembered how I felt then, like I had no power to stop what was happening. I did not want a repeat of 1994. This time, I was going to be part of a solution.

I did what any Generation Xer would in this situation: I went online. After just a few minutes of Googling, I found the Sudan Divestment Task Force.[1] A nonprofit organization founded by college students in California, its entire purpose is to help governments in the United States (and now foreign governments) take action to divest their government funds from companies that help perpetuate the genocide in

Darfur. Looking at the Web site, I felt excited. There was something I could do to impact the genocide! I immediately called the organization's office to learn more. The task force taught me the concept and mechanics of divestment—actively taking steps to divest state pension funds out of those corporations helping the genocide occur and investing that money into corporations that are responsible corporate partners around the world. What a great idea! As a state legislator, I could draft legislation to divest our state pension funds from those companies that provide weapons, oil, and power to the government of Sudan and thereby make it harder for Sudan to carry out its genocide on the people of Darfur.

Divestment was a very exciting idea—until I remembered that I live in Arizona and serve in the Arizona legislature. To say the least, it's not an activist legislature. And the state retirement fund leaders were not at all interested in divestment—in fact, they were opposed to the very concept. I knew I was facing an uphill battle, so I started with education. I held forums at the capitol with Darfuri refugees, showed films about the genocide at the capitol and around the state in schools and churches and synagogues, teamed up with local chapters of Save Darfur and STAND,[2] held a major fund-raiser for Save Darfur, and pestered the media until we got more local coverage of the genocide. I held forums, raised money, met with people, and more, all to gain more Darfur allies. I needed people in the state to support what I was doing, and I needed a lot of them to be willing to talk about Sudan and come to the capitol to help me pass this legislation. Finding support wasn't hard: once people learned about the genocide in Darfur, they wanted to help stop it. Convincing the people I met that they could have a voice at the capitol was another task altogether. We held citizen lobbying workshops all around the state, teaching citizens, students, and Darfuri refugees about the legislative process and how to play a meaningful role in passing legislation.

I also began holding meetings with the Sudan Divestment Task Force and the leaders of our state pension funds to discuss the legislation. I knew that passing a divestment bill wasn't going to be easy. I was planning to sponsor legislation that the pension fund leaders didn't want, and this time the bill would have my name on it. As a Democrat in a Republican legislature, that's a tall order. In the past, I'd always asked Republican colleagues to carry my bills so they'd have a chance of passing. This strategy had worked well over the past three years, and several of my bills became law through the help of a Republican colleague who'd put his or her name on my bill after which we'd work to pass it. But this bill was different. I wanted to carry it myself—and I wanted it to pass. I knew that I would need the support of some influential Republicans, and I knew that I would need the pension fund leaders on my side (or at least not against me).

In our first meeting, the pension fund leaders stated their concerns about divestment and their reasons for opposing it. These were valid concerns that made a lot of sense. For instance, the leaders have a duty to protect the financial integrity of the state pension funds. They can't go off willy-nilly taking money out of some areas and plunking it down into other areas without feeling reasonably secure that citizens' money will be protected. They also weren't thrilled about the idea of the legislature dictating which companies they should and shouldn't invest in; they believed that investment should be a financial decision, not a political one. And finally, they were concerned about efficacy. Would this step actually do something tangible to influence what Is occurring in Sudan, or was it merely a symbolic bill that could cost the funds money without returning any results?

The Sudan Divestment Task Force leaders stated their philosophy of divestment and their method for divesting. Their arguments were valid and made a lot of sense. They cited evidence that divestment *does* make a difference in the behavior of rogue countries, and they had proof that economic "hammers" have made a difference in Sudan in the past. They believe that divestment is a powerful way to stop genocide, even when the federal government of our country and that of other countries, as well as the United Nations, fail to take appropriate physical action to stop the killing. The Sudan Divestment Task Force model had proven to be economically sound, constitutionally fit, and successful in other areas. (In fact, twenty-two states before Arizona divested their state pension funds using the Sudan Divestment Task Force model.) The task force leaders believed that legislatures, as policy-making bodies, have the inherent right to make political decisions about how state investments are made. And finally, they believe that their model protects the financial security of pension funds.

The two groups were about as far apart as two groups could be, and it would have been easy to declare an impasse and move on to the next issue. Instead, we began a nine-month series of meetings, during which we negotiated the terms of the legislation using an *and* strategy instead of a *but* strategy.

My goal was that, at the end, we'd come out of that room with a bill for divestment that everyone could support. The Sudan Divestment Task Force leaders wanted me to use their model legislation because it had proven to be effective in other states and withstood constitutional scrutiny. The model defined how a corporation qualified as a "scrutinized" company—how it was determined that it was a bad actor in Sudan. The pension fund leaders wanted to make their own decisions about which corporations qualified as scrutinized. The Sudan Divestment Task Force leaders would say "We can't support that" and the pension fund leaders would say "We aren't doing this" and I would say "There's got to be a way to get both of these interests met." For months, we struggled through a number of choices about the legisla-tion, and each time it looked like there would be an impasse, we'd look for the *and* option. In the end, we found the *and* option for every portion of the legislation. We drafted legis-lation that included a trigger to protect the financial security of the pension funds. This trigger meant that the pension funds were not mandated to take any action that would lose the funds' money. We modified the definition of *scruti-nized* so that the state pension funds would have more con-trol over deciding which companies to divest from and when to divest. We added a brand new portion to the bill that prohibited the state and its agencies from entering into contracts with corporations that were identified as bad actors in Sudan.

By January 2008 we had a draft bill that I could take to my colleagues in confidence, that the Sudan Divestment Task Force supported, and that the pension fund leaders could live with. Everyone's interests had been met, and we'd achieved our initial goal.

While we were putting the final touches on the bill, I went to a few of my friends in the legislature: Representative Eddie Farnsworth and Representative Andy Biggs. Eddie and Andy are about the most conservative members of the Arizona legislature—in fact, they're about the most conservative people I've ever known. These guys are the real deal. Over the past few years, I'd made friends with Eddie and Andy, much to the consternation of liberals and conservatives alike. While Eddie and Andy are very different from me, they're also funny and smart. We've been able to work together on a number of issues over the past four years, always with pretty decent results. I knew that I could talk to Eddie and Andy about my Sudan legislation and get fair and honest feedback from them. I also knew that if I could get *their* support for my bill, it would be a breeze to get everyone else's. Throughout the fall of 2007, I'd let them know that I was working on a bill and that I'd be asking for their support. They'd been skeptical of the idea of divestment at first because of their philosophical beliefs about using pension funds as a tool for social action, but after talking about the safeguards within the legislation, they warmed to the idea. And after all, we were talking about stopping genocide.

In January, I brought the draft legislation to both guys and asked them to read it and talk to me about any concerns or problems they might have with it. We talked about the bill several times, and they both agreed to sign on. They also helped me talk to other members of the house and senate to garner additional support. By talking to both conservatives and progressives about the bill and earning support from all sides early on, I was able to get every other member of the legislature to sign on to the bill. The bill passed easily through all of its committees, received unanimous support from both the house and the senate, and became the first bill signed by Governor Napolitano in March of 2008.[3]

The Sudan bill taught me the power of *and*, and the importance of my role as a coalition builder in keeping the *and* in the room at all times. When things got tough, as they often did, using *and* kept the Sudan bill alive and led us ultimately to victory.

What were the key actions we took along the way to keep us on the straight and narrow?

• When the going got tough, we stepped back to breathe. I intentionally left large chunks of time between meetings so that we could all get our heads into other projects instead of stewing over the Sudan bill. Then, when we'd come back together after three or four weeks, we could talk about matters from a slightly different and definitely fresher perspective.

• We chose to first find agreement on the "easy" items. This might seem counterintuitive to business (where you might be encouraged to do the nastiest tasks first), but in coalition work, starting with what's easy is key. By finding agreement on the smaller items, you build trust and create a sense of unity. By the time you get to the harder parts, you're all invested in the outcome and want to make it work. If we'd instead started with the toughest point, we would never have gotten the rest of the deal done because it would have blown up right then and there.

• We looked for answers that were not obvious. Rather than forcing ourselves into an either/or situation over language that caused heartburn to one party in the room, we looked for an answer that allowed *both* groups to get what they really wanted (security that the bill would have an impact on Sudan and security that the bill wouldn't bankrupt the retirement system). Being creative with language helped enormously; finding neutral language that neither group was already attached (or opposed) to allowed us all to look at the issue from a different perspective.

The Pitfalls of Using *But* Instead of *And*

The Sudan experience is a nice little story with a very happy ending, but not all stories end like it. There have been plenty of times when I didn't use *and* instead of *but*. These times usually involved me losing. My whole first year in the legislature was mostly *but* not *and*. I'd show up with a bit of moral smugness, feeling very righteous that I alone was crusading for justice by giving a fabulous speech on the floor of the house about this or that most horrible legislation. And then the bill would pass 40–20, or sometimes by even a larger margin. And at the end of the day, all I had was that speech. Which frankly isn't the same as winning.

As a part-time legislator, I have anywhere from three to five additional jobs in order to cover my mortgage and pay the bills. This is common for most legislators around the country, but it sure isn't easy juggling all those jobs. One of my side jobs is practicing law. I pay a lot of attention to legislation that affects our criminal statutes—and as one of the few attorneys in our state legislature, I get a lot of opportunities to see these bills. When I first started in the legislature, I saw a whole lot of bills that I believed were just wrong. The bills made for bad policy and were, in my opinion, poorly written. Some were even unconstitutional. This offended my little lawyer sensibilities, so I'd stand up every couple of days or so on the floor of the house and give a long speech about what was wrong with each bill, complete with references from various cases supporting my view. And then I'd lose. I never even considered walking over to the other side of the room to talk to the House Judiciary Committee *before* these bills passed out of committee to voice my concerns. Oh no, I was much happier giving my speeches and watching the bill pass in front of my eyes.

One example was a bill in 2006 that expanded the aggravating factors to be considered when juries decide whether or not to give the death penalty as a punishment for a person convicted of first-degree murder. This is not a popular topic, and I'm on the least popular side of the question. I'm opposed to the death penalty because I think no civilized society should use it as a punishment. But since we have the death penalty in Arizona, I want to ensure that it's being implemented as fairly and judiciously as possible. When this bill came forward, adding a number of new reasons to put a person to death, I should have gone to the sponsor of the bill and the chair of the House Judiciary Committee to make my case that two of these reasons were written with such broad language that they could, and likely would, be used in cases where they weren't really intended to be used. If I had done a good job of making friends with these two people, I probably could have gotten some of that language adjusted to be a little narrower and truer to the sponsor's intent. But instead, I just gave a fiery speech on the floor of the house. The bill passed and was signed into law.

When you're building a coalition, starting with a ground rule of using *and,* not *but* can infuse the group's work with a philosophy that eschews the old-school black-and-white dichotomy of right and wrong and introduces the new concept that multiple ideas can coexist and actually complement each other in working toward a shared goal. Most importantly, *and* creates the space for people to come together around a common goal and find new, unusual, and interesting ways to accomplish that goal.

Watch for Speed Bumps

I don't know about you, but I have a horrible time with speed bumps. (I hate those new speed tables too.) Perhaps I drive a little faster than I should, but they always seem to creep up out of nowhere, and then the next thing I know, my little Honda Insight is three feet up in the air. They slow me down, jar me out of my driving pattern, and show up when I least expect them! Some might say that I'm just not paying close enough attention to the road (which, given my driving record, is quite possibly accurate), but regardless, they put a real crimp in my style.

Speed bumps happen in coalition work too. They're often there when you least expect them, they jar you out of complacency, and they can threaten your progress if you hit them too hard. Speed bumps hit you when you stop paying attention to your values and interests in creating shared outcomes and slip back into old patterns of operating from positions. They creep into coalition work when you're busy, running out of time, and stressed about the work or outcome you're looking for or anytime things get tough. In progressive coalitions, this means pretty much all the time. We're working against the clock, we don't have enough money, we're all juggling five jobs each, and we're generally facing an uphill battle all the time. The potential for hitting a speed bump is ripe at virtually every moment. Skilled coalition builders are always on the watch for speed bumps and are ready to help guide coalition members over them and back onto safe, productive ground.

Speed bumps occurred throughout our work on the Sudan bill, but we were able to deal with them and continue on the road safely every time. The last speed bump was the toughest because I didn't realize it was coming. Instead, I was wrapped up in driving forward as fast as possible. I needed a little time away from the process to clear my head, and I needed some help to get back on track. The lesson I learned about speed bumps is that they're pretty easy to identify and drive safely over, unless you (the coalition builder) are part of the team that's speeding along too quickly. When that happens, step back and breathe. Ask others for help. Think creatively. And most of all, keep trying. Here's what I mean.

During the drafting of the Sudan divestment bill, we hit speed bumps several times. We'd be going through the bill line by line, and within minutes the tension in the room would escalate as one group said something that pushed another group's buttons. We worked through the early speed bumps. My job as the coalition builder was to (1) notice the speed bump; (2) if I was the one driving us straight into it at full speed, slow down and go back to *and*; and (3) introduce the concept of *and* into the discussion to bring the group back to a productive, engaged discussion. This process worked well for most of our nine months.

Toward the end of our negotiating process, things got hairy. We'd worked through about twelve different parts of the bill, finding middle ground and agreement after lots of negotiation. We continued to hit a brick wall when discussing what the numerical threshold would be to determine when a company was a scrutinized company—a bad actor, if you will. The task force's model legislation said that a company is a bad actor when 5 percent or more of its Sudan-related business is concentrated in the following areas: oil and mineral development and sales, electricity generation, and weapons sales. These are the areas that either directly or indirectly fuel the genocide. The state pension fund leaders wanted to say that a bad actor had to concentrate 5 percent or more of its *total* business in these areas (*total business* meaning all of its business in any part of the world, not just Sudan). The task force refused to accept this idea because it would have exempted the largest bad-actor companies in the world. (They're so big that 5 percent of their business is larger than the whole economy of Sudan!) Under this definition, companies like PetroChina, which definitely helps fund the genocide, would have gotten off scot-free.

For months, I kept avoiding the issue whenever discussions got heated. I'd suggest that we table that issue and move on to another point. But then January came, and the bill was done except for this point. The groups started arguing, the room got tense, the discussion was heated, and I despaired. The meeting ended without a resolution. I talked later with my staff analyst who'd been working on this bill with me for almost a year, and asked him to help me think of a potential solution—a new way to solve this dilemma that didn't involve any *5 percents* anywhere. Several days later, he called with a great idea: instead of arguing about 5 percent of total business versus 5 percent of Sudan-related business, what if we instead said that companies deserved to be labeled as "scrutinized" if they operated *substantial* business in Sudan? This would stop the numbers fight and allow us to focus again on our true goal: to defend those companies helping the genocide succeed. I took the idea, a simple one-word change—the word *substantial*—to the task force and the pension fund leaders, and just like that, the problem was solved. Both parties agreed to the compromise language, and the deal was done. We'd hit a speed bump of technical arguments and creative thinking got us over the bump and back on track.

Recognize that no matter how great your coalition is or how noble your cause is, speed bumps will always pop up during your work. Instead of cursing them, use them as an opportunity to practice your coalition-building skills.

BONUS BOX

And, Not *But* in Practice

Using *and*, not *but* in coalition work gets easier with practice. Just use these tips:

1. **Stop and breathe.** When faced with a new idea that sounds scary, wrong, or frightening, step back and breathe for a moment instead of racing hotly.

2. **Go back to values.** Think about the coalition partner's belief or value underlying this idea. Name it and relate to it.

3. **Reidentify interests.** Talk with your coalition partner about his or her idea, and try to identify the interest that it represents.

4. **Take a time out.** Take some time away from the project if needed. A little time to breathe and clear your mind can help tremendously.

5. **Think outside the box.** Creatively consider how to meet both your interest and your coalition partner's interest. Share your creative ideas with your coalition partner—without claiming attachment to those ideas.

6. **Ask for help.** Enlist outside help if needed. A fresh set of ideas from people who haven't hit the speed bumps you've encountered can open your eyes to new ideas.

11

Keeping the Team Together

Keeping the team together during a campaign can be hard. We're all working eighty hours per week, living off caffeine and chocolate, and everyone gets grumpy and nervous in the weeks leading up to "D-day." Plus, Johnny's mad at Maria for that comment she made in the paper last week, Tracy is worried that Carl's going to use the coalition's e-mail list for his own group's fund-raiser next month, and Kenny doesn't understand why Amber still has a job since she can't manage to make it to more than one coalition meeting in three, and she doesn't do a thing when she does manage to show up. How do you keep everyone on track? I've found that a few key tools can keep the team together and ensure no one ends up on the wrong end of a voodoo pin.

Maintain Accountability

One of the best ways to keep everyone together is through accountability. Building in accountability at the beginning of a coalition's formation is key for a few reasons. First, it starts the group off with a shared commitment to mutual responsibility—everyone is accountable to everyone else, and everyone knows it. Second, it creates a standard for all of you to abide by and measure your activities by, which reduces the fighting later. Third, it allows you to better hold each other accountable down the line because you've all agreed to it in front of each other in a formal way. And finally, it works at the beginning of your coalition's formation because that's when everyone still likes each other and is super excited to be working on this most important project together. (Later, we'll all be a bit less enamored with each other, and we'll be sick and tired of the project, no matter how compelling or exciting it used to be.)

When we started working on the Arizona Together campaign, we knew that it'd be a challenge to keep the coalition together for two years. That's a *long* time to run a campaign, and this was no ordinary campaign. It was a campaign against a difficult social wedge issue, and our coalition was a very diverse and often divergent group. Our core group of ten or twelve people decided that we'd have to build in systems of accountability early on if we wanted to keep the group from ripping apart at the seams. We started by traveling around the state, road-show fashion, to share our early research findings with activists. We solicited feedback and input from people about what kind of campaign (if any) they believed should be run in Arizona. After three or four informational meetings around the state, we got down to business. Several hundred of us gathered in a large meeting hall between Phoenix and Tucson to form a coalition. At that meeting, we used the old Quaker method of consensus decision making when forming our coalition's core principles. Everyone in the room had an equal say in the formation of these principles— unless everyone voted yes on a principle, it wasn't adopted. If someone voted no, he or she bore the responsibility to propose a solution that everyone could support.

The process took forever. Okay, it took only three hours, but it felt like forever! When the air conditioning is out in mid-May in Arizona, even three minutes feels like forever.

At the end of the night, we'd agreed on several core principles:

1. We wanted to win this election. (Because we're progressives, we took care to define what we meant by *win*. Sometimes we define *win* very broadly—including non-numerical wins, like developing a bigger Listserv group or more community awareness or "building the base." For this campaign, we defined *win* as getting more votes than the other guys.)

2. We wanted to use data and research to drive our decision making. (This meant that we weren't going to sit around and decide how the voters felt about same-sex marriage and domestic partnerships; we were going to ask them via polling, listen to the results, and then craft a campaign message targeted to match those results.)

3. We wanted to run a professional campaign. (This meant that we weren't running the campaign out of Bobby's living room, with campaign signs made with three colors of spray paint in Sarah's backyard, using slogans that Jenny wrote on a napkin at Denny's last night.)

These were some pretty serious principles for a brand-new progressive coalition to agree upon. It wasn't easy to get to agreement on the principles, but once completed, the decisions we'd made created a built-in accountability mechanism for all of us. Later, whenever some people wanted to go off the reservation and print up their own signs with homemade slogans and spray paint, the coalition would remind the wayward travelers about those three guiding principles. Our commitment to these guiding principles, and our commitment to holding each other accountable to these principles, kept us focused on the endgame.

Even so, sometimes it was hard to keep the team together. When we completed our first round of research, the data was clear: we needed to talk to voters about how this marriage initiative would hurt unmarried couples. Our campaign workers began talking to unmarried couples throughout the state, learning about what benefits and legal protections they had and what would be taken away if the initiative passed. We talked to the media about these couples and told their stories in our literature and advertising. It was a great strategy, one designed to tell the truth and help voters see the real and immediate consequences of a yes vote.

However, not everyone liked this strategy. Some people within the campaign felt that we shouldn't focus on unmarried couples (especially the straight unmarried ones) and that we should instead talk about the fact that this initiative was discriminatory and that it is wrong to put discrimination into the constitution. Well, it was pretty clear from our research that this line of talk was about the worst kind of talk you could choose in the campaign. We stuck to principle 2 (using data and research to drive our decision making) and held members of our team accountable to that principle. The campaign never used the language that had been so comfortably used and embraced by the LGBT community, despite lots of pressure to do so. And those folks within the campaign who wanted to abandon principle 2 had to choose between their commitment to the campaign's agreed-upon principles or their own desires. Almost everyone chose to be accountable to the principles, and the campaign stayed true to its message through the entire election season.

By using our accountability system and making decisions based on data instead of emotion, we stayed focused on the goal, which was to win more votes on election day. And I'm sure glad that we did because we won that election just months later.

Not every group can use consensus decision making in every situation. I wouldn't even argue that it's the way to work in most situations. But building in a shared accountability system early on, and then tasking every coalition member with the responsibility to be accountable, will keep the team together even when the going gets rough.

Lighten Up, or, No One Likes a Stick in the Mud

Coalitions are hard to form in the first place, and maintaining them takes a yeoman's amount of work and perseverance. But you've got to have a little bit of fun sometime. If you act like a stick in the mud all the time, people will quit the coalition and find something better to do with their time. Fun has to be a conscious part of your work. I don't mean that you need to organize fairs with cotton candy or roller coasters, but you've got to include some room for people to make jokes, be lighthearted, and laugh (both at yourselves and others).

Groups that take themselves too seriously are boring and stuffy, and no one wants to be anywhere near them. You know these so-called coalitions. They're the ones run by the Most Dedicated Activist in the World, and you really shouldn't even bother attending the meetings because you're clearly a Corporate Sellout Who Doesn't Care About Anything. Even the air in these meetings is stifling. These groups may start out with a coalition-like tendency—diverse people, a large group, and so on. But within a few months, it's turned into the West Bay Peace Activists for the Protection and Liberation of Oppressed Peoples in Moldova, with a group membership of six. And if you're not wearing all-hemp clothing, listening to Cat Stevens, and making your own paper and soy ink, you are not welcome, which isn't a problem for you because you don't want to work with those stiffs anyway. The truth is this: yes, there is no more important time in our country's history than now, and our good work is needed more than at any time in the past, but still, no one likes a humorless and rigid activist.

To avoid falling into the trap of taking yourself too seriously, I recommend that you set an atmosphere of coalition work that is intent on reaching the group's shared goal (because that's why you're all at the table together, after all) and also respects and appreciates people's foibles, funny stories, and good humor. One way to ensure that you have a coalition that is fun is to include people who know how to have fun. If you've done a good job making friends, these people will be easy to find and collect around you. After you invite these fun and funny people to join you in the coalition, start the group's work with an attitude that invites some humor. I always build in a few minutes of premeeting time (five to ten minutes) to let people around the table catch up and have a little fun together. Keep in mind that some people aren't so good at this. They will at first get tense when others have fun, or even insert rigid comments designed to pick a little fight with the person across the table who is different from them. And that's why it's really important for you to be there—you can defuse this situation and set an example for the other coalition members that blending important, serious work with a little bit of good humor not only is acceptable, it's encouraged. Over time, the rigid ones will realize that it's okay to have a little fun and that fun and work can and should go hand in hand.

Say It Straight

I'm a big fan of honesty. I think it's generally the way to go. People want politicians to be honest (while at the same time expecting every word they say to be a big fat lie). My problem is that sometimes I'm too honest. As your mother undoubtedly told you, sometimes it's best to say nothing at all if you can't say anything nice. I'm working on that one. But telling the truth is a biggie.

Whether you've formed a small coalition with one other person or a large coalition of one hundred, trust has to be at the foundation of your working relationship. Without trust, you don't have a coalition. You have a tightrope. And there's no room on a tightrope to find solutions to your shared problems.

Why trust and honesty? The answer seems pretty simple to me: if other people think that you're not on the up-and-up, then they're not going to put their cards on the table. And since the fundamentals of coalition work include letting go of outcomes, agreeing on shared values, and setting up plans of action together, getting the cards on the table is pretty important.

I thought of a whole bunch of stories that would make my point, but the simple fact is that I'm still a sitting legislator, and telling stories about people whom I've worked with who weren't telling it straight is political suicide. So I'll leave it at this: you know how it feels when someone doesn't tell the truth, and you've seen the destruction that occurs when dishonesty is the name of the game.

BONUS BOX

Keepin' It Together

Here are three steps to keep moving—even when the going gets rough.

1. **Maintain accountability.** Set up guiding principles, rules, or whatever you want to call them. Then stick to them, and expect others in the coalition to do so too.

2. **Lighten up.** Have some fun. Laugh. Sometimes, laugh at yourself.

3. **Say it straight.** Be honest and trustworthy. You want to believe in and trust others in the group, so make sure you carry that same expectation of yourself.

 **CONCLUSION**

Get Your Coalition On

W e're almost done here. We started on this little journey with a quick look at the world we've got and the world we want. We know that we're not quite in the world we want, so what do we do? As political actors, we need to stop the pettiness and the meanness and the sneaky strategy and instead practice politics under a new ethos—one where people are genuine and are open to new ideas and possibilities and where smear attacks and nasty innuendo-filled commercials have no place.

We learned that it's hard to reach this goal unless we take some time to change the way that we personally think and behave. While changing our own thoughts and emotions and behaviors isn't easy, taking time to notice ourselves and then choosing to change can steer us in the direction of our new ethos.

As humans, we like to work together. We recognize that we're more powerful and productive as a collective, so we tend to create and maintain coalitions to achieve our goals. Sometimes our coalitions become boring or fraught with tension or even devolve into uselessness. When we create coalitions that are diverse, purposeful, and driven with leadership, we can achieve great things.

It's time for us to consider letting go of the identities that have defined us in the past. Today, we recognize that we're all in this world together and that actions to benefit or hurt one group of people really benefit or hurt us all. We can shift our work to include a broader definition of us and free ourselves from the limiting circles of silos. Once we've freed ourselves from the limiting definitions of identity politics, we're ready to form relationships with people and groups outside of our comfort zone. By learning to make friends with new people, people who are different from ourselves, we open up the creative possibilities for great political work.

Shifting the way that we think and talk to each other in coalitions can create excellent opportunities for collective action. When we let go of our attachment to specific outcomes and instead focus on our shared values, we can think creatively about solutions to the many problems we face today. Articulating our interests, rather than our positions, creates the space for each of us to consider new alternatives, new options, and new ways to reach our collective goal. And when we're open to the possibility of new ideas and new solutions, we can achieve more than we ever could acting alone.

Nothing is more powerful than a group of people who've come together of their own free will, determined to address a problem, with a dedication to each other and to truth and with a belief in the collective power of people. Using the principles of coalition work that I've discussed in this book, I believe, will help us on our journey to transform our nation and our planet. We all have dreamed of a better world. Most of us have been working for that better world throughout our lives. Now, more than ever, we must join together in new, creative, and expansive ways to get closer to that world we're dreaming of. My hope for each of you (and for myself) is that the experiences shared, lessons learned, and truths I've articulated in this book make our journey a little smoother.

BONUS RESOURCE

The
Coalition
Builder's
Toolkit

Talking about coalition building is great. The task always seems so easy when you read about it, but doing it can be very hard. This toolkit provides some handy tips for actually creating and maintaining a coalition that's designed to win. Written as a complement to the book, it can also serve as a stand-alone tool for readers and doers on the go. The toolkit uses the Arizona Together experience as a guide for you in real life.

The three key elements to a winning strategy are research, truth, and discipline. They're simple and clear, and that's why I like them. Plus, they work really, really well.

Research

We progressives are really smart. We're great at the facts— we know them all and often recite them to a very bored audience—but we're horrible at figuring out what others want to hear. We think that all people want to hear what we want to say. But they don't. And that's what research is for.

Research in an electoral campaign is very simply the polling and focus-group work that strategic campaigns engage in *before* they start a campaign and learn from during the campaign. Data gleaned from polls and focus groups can tell you whether you've got a fighting chance to win or whether you might want to consider opening a bakery instead. Research can tell you what kind of issues are important to voters at a given time and what they just don't care about.

Research can help you see what people in another city or region of the country think about your brilliant ideas for economic development, and it can tell you if people have never heard about the consequences of a proposed policy change. Research helps you get access to the thoughts and, most importantly, the emotions of the voters who will be deciding what they think about your issue or candidate.

Often, our coalitions run short on cash. As a result, we sometimes skip this part of a campaign, thinking, "Well, we just don't have the money for research." This is a really big mistake because it's then entirely possible (and often quite probable) that you'll spend the little money you *do* have in your campaign saying all the wrong things to the voters.

Sometimes, progressives think that research is inherently bad. You'll hear people say, "We don't do polls. We just speak the truth." Well, everything everyone says is *someone's* truth, so that's not a very useful statement. Research helps you find out which truths matter most to the voters and what language voters can hear the best. When you conduct good research, you will learn how to frame your message (that's fancy for "how you talk about something") in a way that voters can hear you.

I've become a huge fan of research. It's helped me as a candidate learn to talk in ways that voters can understand. For example, I used to say that I wanted universal health-care coverage in Arizona, which went over like a ton of bricks. Turns out, Arizonans hear the word *universal* and think *socialism*—or *pinko commie*. But when I say that I want all Arizonans to have access to affordable, quality health care,

Arizonans agree wholeheartedly. Same basic idea, different language. Research is what teaches us these differences so that we can relate to voters in ways that are authentic and meaningful for them.

Truth

Truth is perhaps our greatest strength. As progressives, we are dedicated to the truth. We love to tell it, we love to hear it, and we love to feel justified by it. Problem is, no one ever taught us how to tell the truth in a way that allows most others to hear it. One thing I've learned the hard way is to always tell the truth—but perhaps not using a bullhorn on the side of the street.

We progressives get mad when we see politicians and campaigns lying because *it's just wrong to lie*. This we can all agree on: it's wrong to lie. It's also wrong to tell half-truths and be sneaky about the truth—no doubt about it. But we can be strategic in the way that we communicate the truth. We don't have to be rude or mean about the truth. We don't have to call others names (even if they're well deserved). We don't have to cite *every* fact and figure that exists to back up our claims. We can tell a clean, simple truth that uses language that voters understand and that resonates with them.

We can stay true to our progressive values (that's easy because we all share pretty much the same values) and tell the truth about what we care about without needlessly ticking people off. For instance, we can say that we're against a ban on same-sex marriage without using a campaign strategy that says "Dear Bigot Voters: Please Don't Write Discrimination into the Constitution." That's about the worst statement you could make, especially when you can say lots of great and important truths about these marriage bans in less offensive, more engaging ways—for instance, by focusing on privacy or fairness or family—things we all care about. We can tell the truth to voters without being offensive or calling people names.

In 2008, I was lucky to lead Protect Arizona's Freedom, the coalition formed to stop Ward Connerly, the California millionaire who goes around the country trying to eliminate equal opportunity programs. Connerly came to Arizona, but because of fraud and illegal signature gathering, he failed to get his initiative on the ballot. Before that failure, though, we spent quite a bit of time talking to Arizona voters about this proposed initiative. Connerly promoted it as the "Arizona Civil Rights Initiative" and said that it would end discrimination in the state. In truth, however, the measure had nothing to do with civil rights and would actually have eliminated all equal opportunity programs in Arizona that benefit women and people of color. We set out to let Arizona voters know what these programs were and who would be hurt if the initiative passed, and we did it by telling the stories of people who are enrolled in the affected college programs and what the programs do for people in our state. Turns out, people in Arizona don't like the idea of eliminating programs that help support women earning degrees in science and math. They also don't like the idea of eliminating programs that help women who are survivors of domestic violence.

By simply telling the truth about these programs and the people who would be hurt if they were eliminated, we were able to talk about Connerly's initiative in a way that mattered to voters and made a difference in their minds.

Discipline

The Right is a discipline machine, which is one of the major reasons that conservatives have been so successful in recent history. Progressives, on the other hand, are a little more free-flowing. We all have our own ideas and want to share them with the world, and, oh—look at that shiny penny!

Because we're so smart and creative and we care about everything, we tend to have trouble staying focused on one issue or topic or campaign at a time. We may be personally able to handle the fast-moving pace between sentences and thoughts, but the *voters* cannot. They are really busy with the rest of their lives, and they want one good message at a time from you, thank you very much. Give more than that, and they will vote for the other guy.

This is where message discipline comes in. When you've done your research and determined what truths the voters can hear, then your job is to tell them that truth and not clutter it up with your other 15 million great ideas. Just tell them what you'd like them to know about this important issue or this specific candidate, and then *get out of the way*. The coalitions that do this are wildly successful because they've learned what advertisers have known all along: people want to get the information they need to make an informed decision, and then they want you to get out of the way while they make their decision.

Remember, less is more. Find your one or two key truths—messages that resonate with your target audience   and say those one or two key truths over and over. Resist the temptation to cite sixteen sources during your spiel. No one cares about your sixteen sources. Also resist the temptation to talk for forty-five minutes. No one wants to hear you talk for forty-five minutes (except maybe your mom, but that's just because she loves you so much). And finally, resist the temptation to continue adding more reasons that the voters should agree with you—they stopped listening after number two. Just find your one or two key points via good research, say them well, say them over and over, and don't give in to the itch of embellishment. This is not home decorating—you do not need a flourish. Winning is the best flourish of all.

NOTES

Introduction

1. Basically, he told me to sit down and shut up. I smirked and stood up to give another fiery speech.

2. It's sure not the money. They pay us in peanuts. Well, they actually pay in dollars, but sometimes I think pay in peanuts might be more valuable.

Chapter 1

1. Lee Hamilton, "Why Is Congress So Partisan?" Lee Hamilton Commentaries, The Center on Congress at Indiana University, http://www.centeroncongress.org/radio_commentaries/why_is_congress_so_partisan.php.

2. James G. Gimpel, *Fulfilling the Contract: The First 100 Days* (Boston: Allyn & Bacon, 1996), 8.

3. "Obama Claims Big Win in South Carolina," CNN, January 27, 2008. http://www.cnn.com/2008/POLITICS/01/26/sc.primary/index.html.

4. Chris Markham, "Chandler Wants Nursing Moms to Cover Up," *East Valley Tribune*, August 9, 2005, http://www.eastvalleytribune.com/story/45858.

5. A really effective way to influence legislation is to build a big farm team of ordinary people throughout the state who are willing to send e-mails and make phone calls to their legislators supporting or opposing a bill. When a legislator sees hundreds of people e-mailing and calling about a specific issue, he or she knows that a lot of people care about this issue and are paying attention to what the legislator does. It really does change how legislators behave.

6. For instance, I can't cook a thing. I did turn on the oven once a few years ago, but can't remember exactly why. It certainly didn't result in a tasty, home-cooked meal.

Chapter 2

1. W. B. Cannon, *Bodily Changes in Pain, Hunger, Fear and Rage: An Account of Recent Researches into the Function of Emotional Excitement* (New York: Appleton, 1915).

2. "The Serenity Now," *Seinfeld*, episode 159, first broadcast October 9, 1997, on NBC, directed by Andy Ackerman and written by Steve Koren.

3. *See generally* Robert Fried, *Breathe Well, Be Well: A Program to Relieve Stress, Anxiety, Asthma, Hypertension, Migraine, and Other Disorders for Better Health* (New York: John Wiley & Sons, 1999).

Chapter 3

1. David Holthouse, "Arizona Showdown: High-Powered Firearms, Militia Maneuvers and Racism at the Minuteman Project," *Intelligence Report* 118 (2005).

2. Pew Hispanic Center, "Arizona: Population and Labor Force Characteristics, 2000–2006," January 23, 2008, http://pewhispanic.org/factsheets/factsheet.php?Fact sheetID=37; and U.S. Census Bureau, "Louisiana Loses Population; Arizona Edges Nevada as Fastest-Growing State," U.S. Census Bureau News, December 22, 2006, http://www.census.gov/Press-Release/www/releases/ archives/population/007910.html.

3. *Border Protection, Antiterrorism, and Illegal Immigration Control Act of 2005*, HR 4437, 100th Cong., introduced on December 6, 2005, passed by the U.S. House of Representatives on December 16, 2005. Description of bill available at http://thomas.loc.gov/cgi-bin/bdquery/ z?d109:HR04437:@@@L&summ2=m&. Text of legislation available at http://thomas.loc.gov/cgi-bin/query/ z?c109:H.R.4437.

4. Allan Chernoff, "Rallies Across U.S. Call for Illegal Immigrant Rights," CNN.com, April 10, 2006, http:// www.cnn.com/2006/POLITICS/04/10/immigration/ index.html.

5. Author discussions with Phoenix Police Department, Arizona Capitol Police, and Arizona Department of Public Safety.

6. President George W. Bush, "President Urges Readiness and Patience," Camp David, September 15, 2001, text of speech available at http://www.whitehouse.gov/ news/releases/2001/09/20010915-4.html.

7. President George W. Bush, "The President's State of the Union Address," United States Capitol, January 29, 2002,

text of speech available at http://www.whitehouse
.gov/news/releases/2002/01/20020129-11.html.

8. *Operation King's Dream v. Connerly*, No. 06-12773, 2006
U.S. Dist. LEXIS 61323 (E.D. Mich. Aug. 29, 2006); Jocelyn
Friedrichs Benson, "Election Fraud and the Initiative
Process: A Study of the 2006 Michigan Civil Rights
Initiative" *Fordham Urban Law Journal* 34, no. 3 (2007),
889–934, available at http://law.fordham.edu/ihtml/
page3g_nob.ihtml?imac=1264&pubID=400&article
id=2421; "State Anti-Affirmative Action Petition Drive
Draws Criticism," *Oklahoman*, February 21, 2008;
"Affirmative Action Supporters Call Drive Misleading,"
Kansas City Star, April 1, 2008; and M. Susan Savage,
Oklahoma Secretary of State, letter to Oklahoma
Supreme Court Chief Justice James Winchester,
February 7, 2008, available at http://www.stop
ballotfraud.org/merchant/national_ballot_access/.

9. "Petition Backers Indicted on Felony Charges," *NewsOK*,
October 2, 2007, http://newsok.com/article/3138948/
1191354365.

10. Seth Colter Wells, "Affirmative Action Ban Likely to Be
Striped from Arizona Ballot, Opponents Say," *Huffington
Post*, August 19, 2008, http://www.huffingtonpost
.com/2008/08/19/affirmative-action-ban-li_n_119831
.html.

Chapter 4

1. Carolyn Szczepanski, "A College Drop-Out Abandons a
Lucrative Tech Career for a Life of Inner-City

Poverty—and Hopes to Save an Urban School District from Oblivion," *Pitch Kansas City*, February 19, 2008, http://www.pitch.com/2008-02-21/news/the-teacher/.

2. Airick Leonard West, interview by author, May 31, 2008.

3. "Unity," Kansas Citians United for Educational Achievement, http://www.kcu4ea.org/unity.php.

4. Whitney Terrell, "City Mule, Country Mule," *New York Times*, March 23, 2008, http://www.nytimes.com/2008/03/23/opinion/23terrell.html.

5. I should note here that I myself am a member of the LGBT community. And I promise you that I do not like pain, so throwing myself under a bus is not so much my style.

Chapter 5

1. Molly Ivins, "Molly Ivins February 21," creators.com, February 21, 1999, http://www.creators.com/opinion/molly-ivins/molly-ivins-february-21-1999-02-21.html.

2. Karen Johnson, "Backing My Claims About 9/11 Questions," *East Valley (AZ) Tribune*, May 2, 2008, http://www.eastvalleytribune.com/story/115376.

3. Richard Ruelas, "Karen Johnson: Life in the Legislature," *Arizona Republic*, July 16, 2008, http:// www.azcentral.com/arizonarepublic/arizonaliving/articles/2008/07/16/20080716karenjohnson0716.html.

4. "Bill Richardson's Diplomacy," *Denver Post*, September 15, 2006, http://www.denverpost.com/opinion/ci_434 0173.

5. "Presidential Candidate Bill Richardson Arrives in North Korea," *USA Today*, April 8, 2007, http://www.usatoday .com/news/washington/2007-04-08-nkorea-remains_N .htm.

6. Bill Richardson, interview by Margaret Warner, *Online News Hour*, PBS, December 11, 1996, transcript available at http://www.pbs.org/newshour/bb/africa/ december96/richardson_12-11.html.

7. Douglas Waller, Tamala M. Edwards, and Scott Macleod, "Bail Bondsman to the World," *Time*, December 23, 1996, http://www.time.com/time/magazine/article/0,9171 ,985724,00.html.

8. Bill Richardson, *Between Worlds: The Making of an American Life* (New York: G. P. Putnam's Sons, 2005).

9. Sarah Lynch, "Pearce Calls on 'Operation Wetback' for Illegals," *East Valley (AZ) Tribune*, September 29, 2006, http://www.eastvalleytribune.com/story/75335.

10. *Fight Club*, Fox Movies, 1999, http://www.foxmovies .com/fightclub/.

Chapter 6

1. All information and quotes in this story are from Jeremy Kalin, interview by author, June 3, 2008.

2. National Geographic, "Gateway Community Toolkit," Center for Sustainable Destinations, http://www

.nationalgeographic.com/travel/sustainable/gateway
_community_toolkit.html.

3. David Fulmer, interview by author, July 17, 2008.

Chapter 7

1. All information in this story is from Garrick Delzell, interview by author, September 24, 2008.

2. Barack Obama, Democratic National Convention Acceptance Speech, August 28, 2008, text of speech available at http://www.demconvention.com/barack -obama/.

3. I think we can eventually find that area where agreement is possible if we keep trying. It's not easy to keep trying, though, and sometimes we decide (rightfully so) that our efforts would be better used elsewhere.

Chapter 8

1. Crissie McMullan, interview by author, June 30, 2008, Grow Montana http://www.growmontana.ncat.org/.

2. *Montana Food to Institutions*, SB 328, 2007, detailed bill information available at http://laws.leg.mt.gov/laws07/ LAW0210W$BSIV.ActionQuery?P_BILL_NO1=328&P _BLTP_BILL_TYP_CD=SB&Z_ACTION=Find.

3. *Value-Added Food Production Study*, SJ 13, 2007, detailed bill information available at http://laws.leg.mt .gov/laws07/1 AW0210W$BSIVActionQuery?P_BILL _NO1=13&P_BLTP_BILL_TYP_CD=SJ&Z_ACTION=Find.

4. *Resolution to Remove Ban on Interstate Commerce of State-Inspected Meat*, HJ 17, 2007, detailed bill information available at http://laws.leg.mt.gov/laws07/LAW02 03W$BSRV.ActionQuery?P_BLTP_BILL_TYP_CD=HJ&P _BILL_NO=17&P_BILL_DFT_NO=&P_CHPT_NO=&Z _ACTION=Find&P_SBJ_DESCR=Agriculture++(see +also%3A+Livestock%3B+Taxation—Agriculture%2F Livestock)&P_SBJT_SBJ_CD=AGR&P_LST_NM1=&P _ENTY_ID_SEQ=.

Chapter 9

1. I don't mean *Third Way* as in the Bill Clinton Third Way. I mean *Third Way* as in a new way of working together. Not that there's anything wrong with Bill Clinton's Third Way. This is just different.

2. Mark Wendelsdorf, interview by author, July 18, 2008.

Chapter 10

1. For more information, see http://www.sudan divestment.org.

2. Save Darfur is a national nonprofit coalition of over 170 groups working to end the genocide in Darfur. For more information, see http://www.savedarfur.org. STAND (formerly Students Taking Action Now: Darfur) is the student-led division of the genocide prevention network. For more information, see http://www .standnow.org.

3. *Sudan; Investments; Business Operations; Prohibition,*
   HB 2705, 48th Legislature, Second Regular Session,
   detailed bill information available at http://www.azleg
   .gov/FormatDocument.asp?inDoc=/legtext/48leg/2r/
   bills/hb2705o.asp.

ACKNOWLEDGMENTS

I would like to first express my gratitude to life for giving me all the wonderful opportunities I've had to grow and learn, and extend my apologies for any and all of the times that I squandered those opportunities. May I do so less in the future.

Thank you to those who've journeyed with me on the road from starry-eyed idealist to (still) starry-eyed pragmatist: Chad Campbell, who believed in me from the beginning and even quit lucrative jobs to join me on this wild ride called politics; David Lujan, who never once has complained about my big mouth or bossy ways and is the best teammate ever; Sandy Bahr, for having coffee with me that day and for every time since; and Regina Jefferies, Sanja Bogdanovic, and Stefanie Sidortsova for skipping law school classes to get me elected and for being the best friends a girl could ever have. Long live the coven.

I would like to thank Cynthia Leigh Lewis, Kendra Leiby, and Cynthia Aragon for always answering my calls and saying yes. The work is so much easier with you all there! Thanks to Steve May for soldiering through Arizona Together with me. Special thanks to my aunt Sandra, who is the best social worker I've ever met and who taught me what's really important in life.

This book wouldn't be nearly as interesting without the stories that others generously shared with me—thank you to David Fulmer, Crissie McMullen, Garrick Delzell, Airick Leonard West, Jeremy Kalin, and Mark Wendelsdorf. And life wouldn't be nearly as interesting without the people whom I've been lucky to make friends with and create coalitions with here in Arizona and around the nation—thank you all. Thank you to all the great and powerful groups around the nation that have supported me, promoted me, and helped me over the years— they know how much I love this work and graciously let me talk about it at meetings the world over.

Special thanks is lavished upon my editor, Johanna Vondeling, who offered me this amazing opportunity and helped me realize it. This book would have rolled around in my head for decades if not for her. Abundant thanks also goes to managing editor, Jeevan Sivasubramaniam, who never once threatened to kill me for missing deadlines, although I often deserved it, and who introduced me to the joy of Iphone applications. I am so grateful to everyone at Berrett-Koehler for taking such great care of me and this little book. Thanks to Tai Moses, Rob Ellman, and Safir Ahmed for their insightful and kind feedback. A huge thank you to Janet Napolitano for reading my book and writing the foreword in the midst of moving to Washington, DC, to keep our country safe and secure.

And finally, thank you to all the many people who are working to make our planet more just every day. As Martin Luther King, Jr., said, "The arc of the universe is long, but it curves toward justice." Thank you for working on the curve.

INDEX

ABOUT THE AUTHOR

I n 2004, Kyrsten Sinema—activist, organizer, and accomplished troublemaker—put down her homemade protest signs and ran for the Arizona State Legislature. She has since served two terms in the house, was recently elected to a third term, and now serves as the assistant leader to the house Democrats. After some initial bumps and bruises, Kyrsten figured out how to successfully navigate state politics and thereby deliver real results that serve her constituents.

Kyrsten's path to politics was unusual. She began her professional career in 1995 as a social worker in the Sunnyslope community of Phoenix. Over the next eight years, she created and directed a family resource center, focusing her work on community development and empowerment. In 2002, she decided to earn a law degree and run for public office, which led to her current service in the state legislature.

Kyrsten's favorite activity is talking about politics. Since 2003, she has taught future organizers, activists, and political actors about government, politics, fund-raising, and social policy at the School of Social Work at Arizona State University (her alma mater), and she's delighted to see former students working for social justice around the country. She is also privileged to teach political skills to Arizonans

eager to create progressive policy at the Center for Progressive Leadership. Kyrsten tries not to practice law, but
when she does, she specializes in criminal defense, immigration, and election law. She has been quite gratified to receive
numerous awards over the years for her political impact in
local, state, and national arenas.

Kyrsten is particularly fascinated by the initiative and referendum process and works on ballot issues in Arizona and
around the country. In 2006, she chaired Arizona Together,
the first and only successful campaign to defeat a same-sex
marriage ban, and in 2008, she ran Protect Arizona's Freedom, which successfully kept Ward Connerly's anti–equal
opportunity initiative off the state ballot.

She is frequently asked to consult on progressive political
efforts around the country and to speak to groups nation-
wide on a variety of topics she cares about. She's happiest
when a speech or talk inspires other people to act and work
together in new ways and is always excited to see people
forming coalitions and engaging politically.

Kyrsten lives in Phoenix. She is currently pursuing a PhD at
Arizona State University's School of Justice and Social Inquiry,
focusing on the history of armed warfare and genocide in
Africa. She is an avid reader, hikes her favorite mountain
every day, and never passes up a chance to go shopping.

• About Berrett-Koehler Publishers

Berrett-Koehler is an independent publisher dedicated to an ambitious mission: **Creating a World That Works for All.**

We believe that to truly create a better world, action is needed at all levels—individual, organizational, and societal. At the individual level, our publications help people align their lives with their values and with their aspirations for a better world. At the organizational level, our publications promote progressive leadership and management practices, socially responsible approaches to business, and humane and effective organizations. At the societal level, our publications advance social and economic justice, shared prosperity, sustainability, and new solutions to national and global issues.

A major theme of our publications is "Opening Up New Space." They challenge conventional thinking, introduce new ideas, and foster positive change. Their common quest is changing the underlying beliefs, mindsets, institutions, and structures that keep generating the same cycles of problems, no matter who our leaders are or what improvement programs we adopt.

We strive to practice what we preach—to operate our publishing company in line with the ideas in our books. At the core of our approach is stewardship, which we define as a deep sense of responsibility to administer the company for the benefit of all of our "stakeholder" groups: authors, customers, employees, investors, service providers, and the communities and environment around us.

We are grateful to the thousands of readers, authors, and other friends of the company who consider themselves to be part of the "BK Community." We hope that you, too, will join us in our mission.

A BK Currents Book

This book is part of our BK Currents series. BK Currents books advance social and economic justice by exploring the critical intersections between business and society. Offering a unique combination of thoughtful analysis and progressive alternatives, BK Currents books promote positive change at the national and global levels. To find out more, visit www.bkcurrents.com.

• Be Connected

Visit Our Website

Go to www.bkconnection.com to read exclusive previews and excerpts of new books, find detailed information on all Berrett-Koehler titles and authors, browse subject-area libraries of books, and get special discounts.

Subscribe to Our Free E-Newsletter

Be the first to hear about new publications, special discount offers, exclusive articles, news about bestsellers, and more! Get on the list for our free e-newsletter by going to www .bkconnection.com.

Get Quantity Discounts

Berrett-Koehler books are available at quantity discounts for orders of ten or more copies. Please call us toll-free at (800) 929-2929 or email us at bkp.orders@aidcvt.com.

Host a Reading Group

For tips on how to form and carry on a book reading group in your workplace or community, see our website at www .bkconnection.com.

Join the BK Community

Thousands of readers of our books have become part of the "BK Community" by participating in events featuring our authors, reviewing draft manuscripts of forthcoming books, spreading the word about their favorite books, and supporting our publishing program in other ways. If you would like to join the BK Community, please contact us at bkcommunity@bkpub.com.